I0499376

The best Coloring book

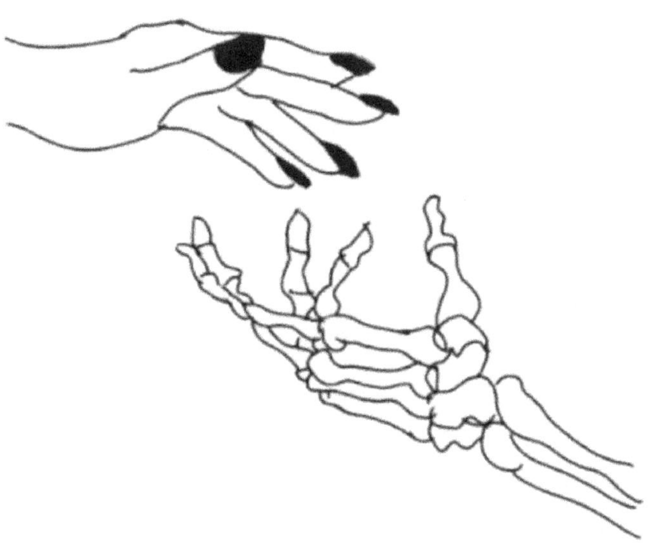

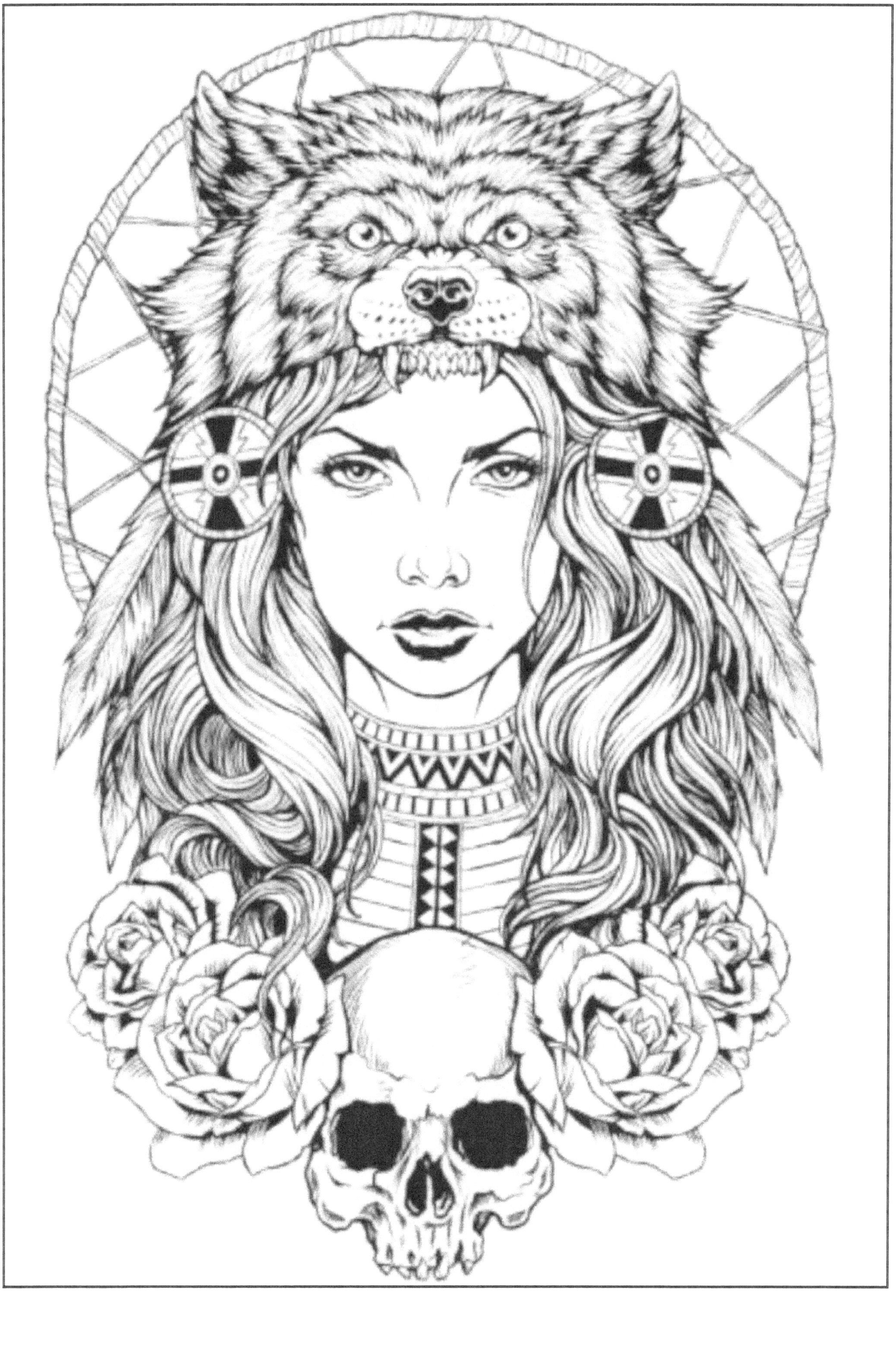

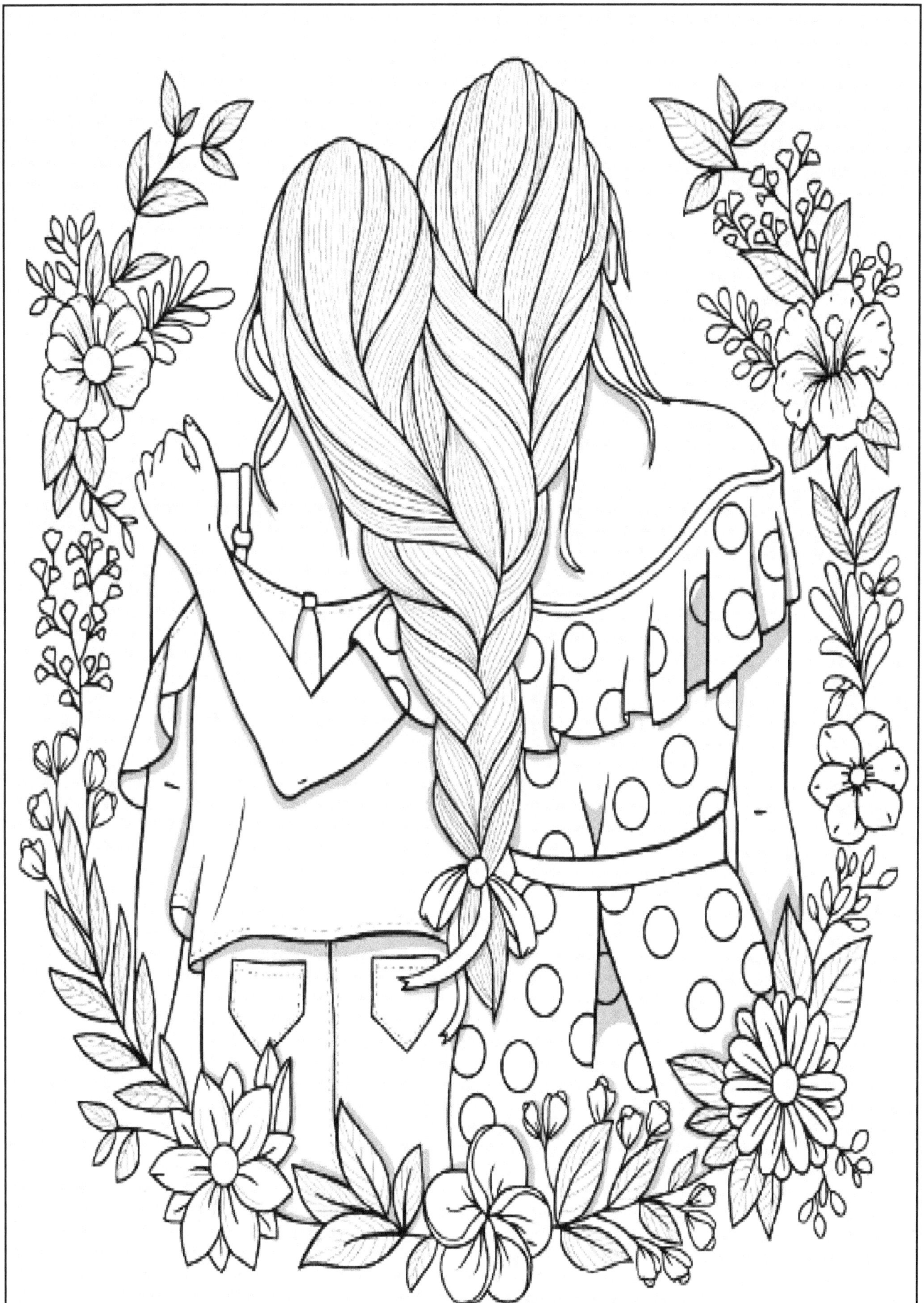

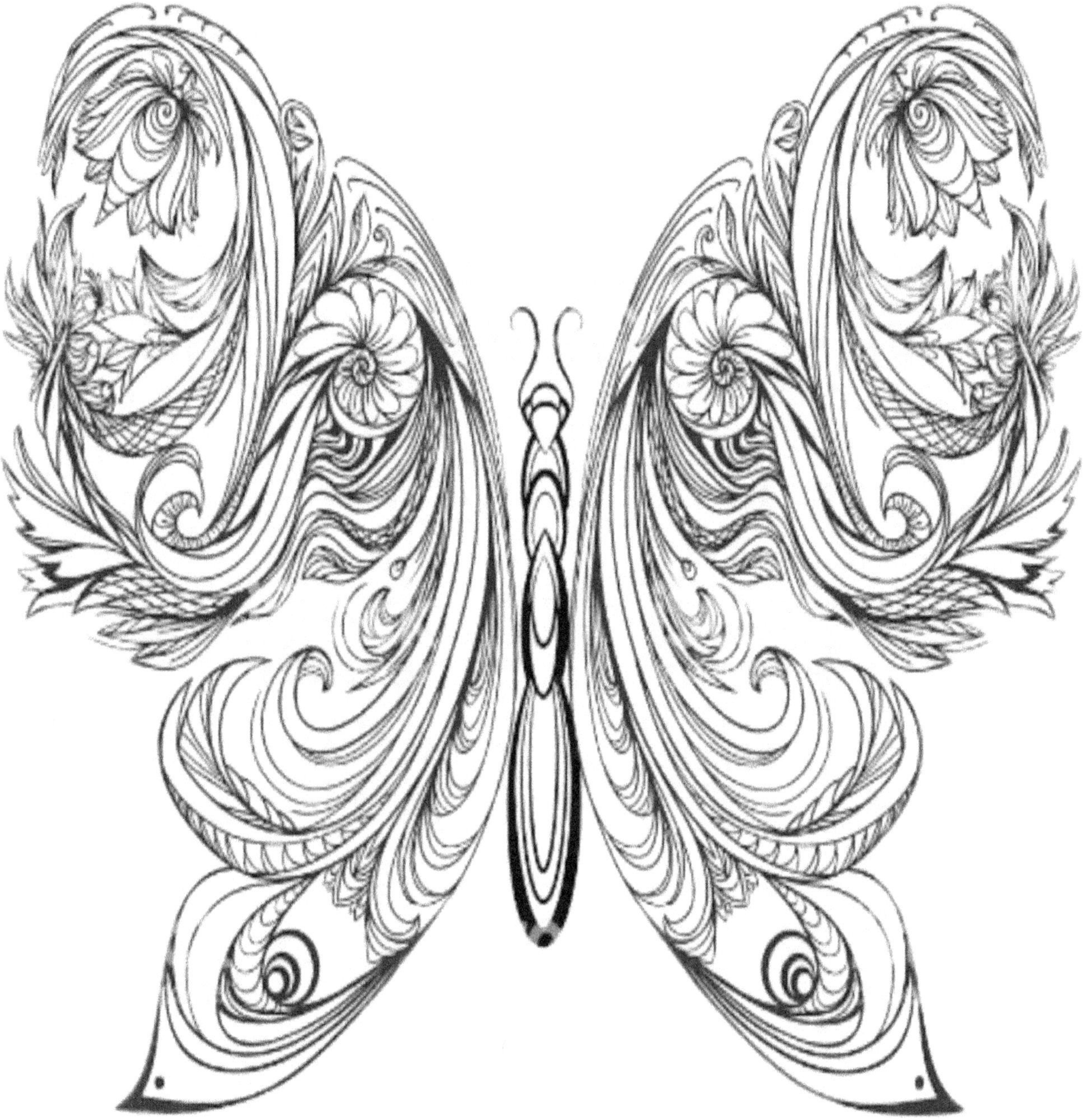

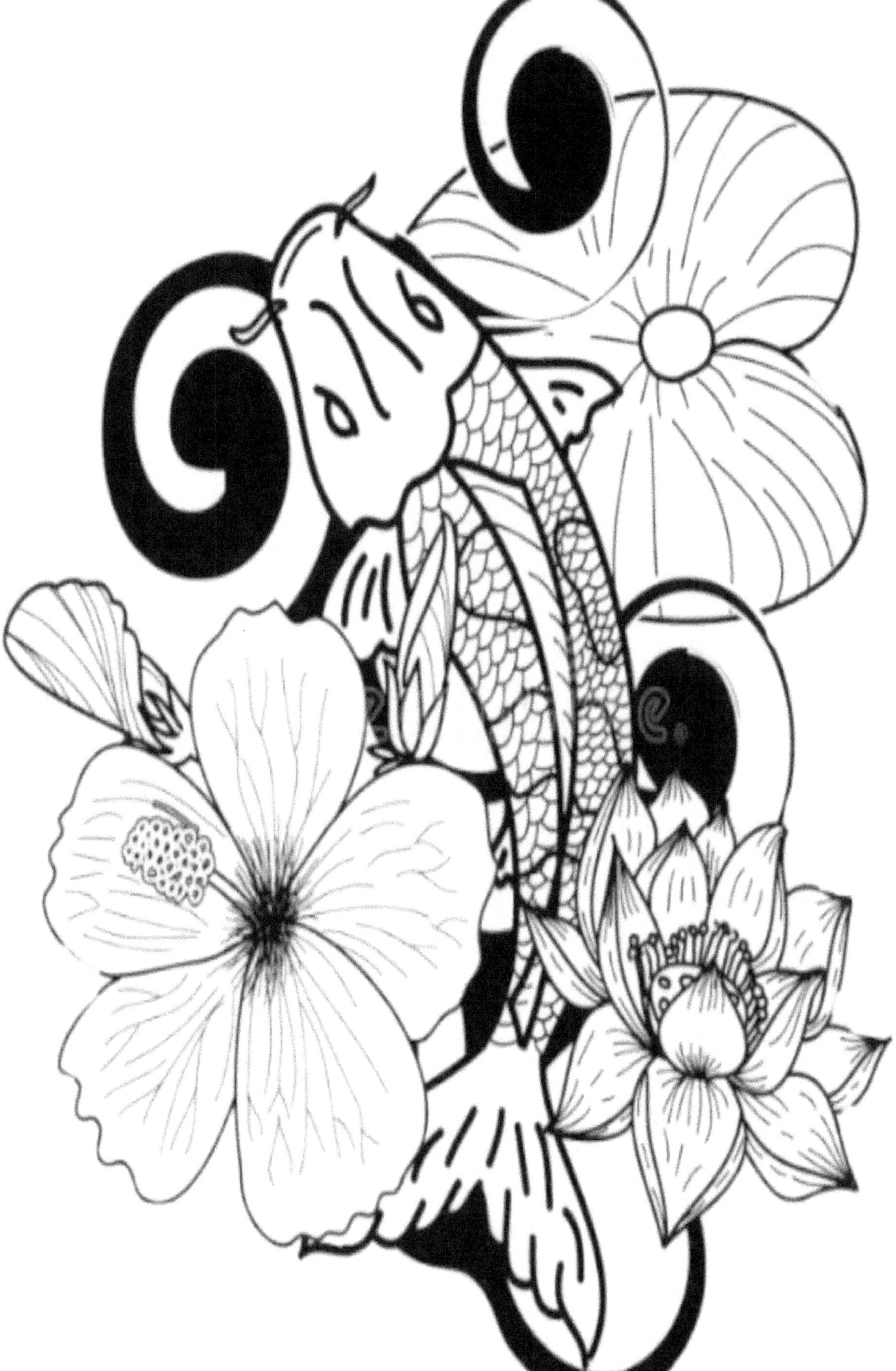

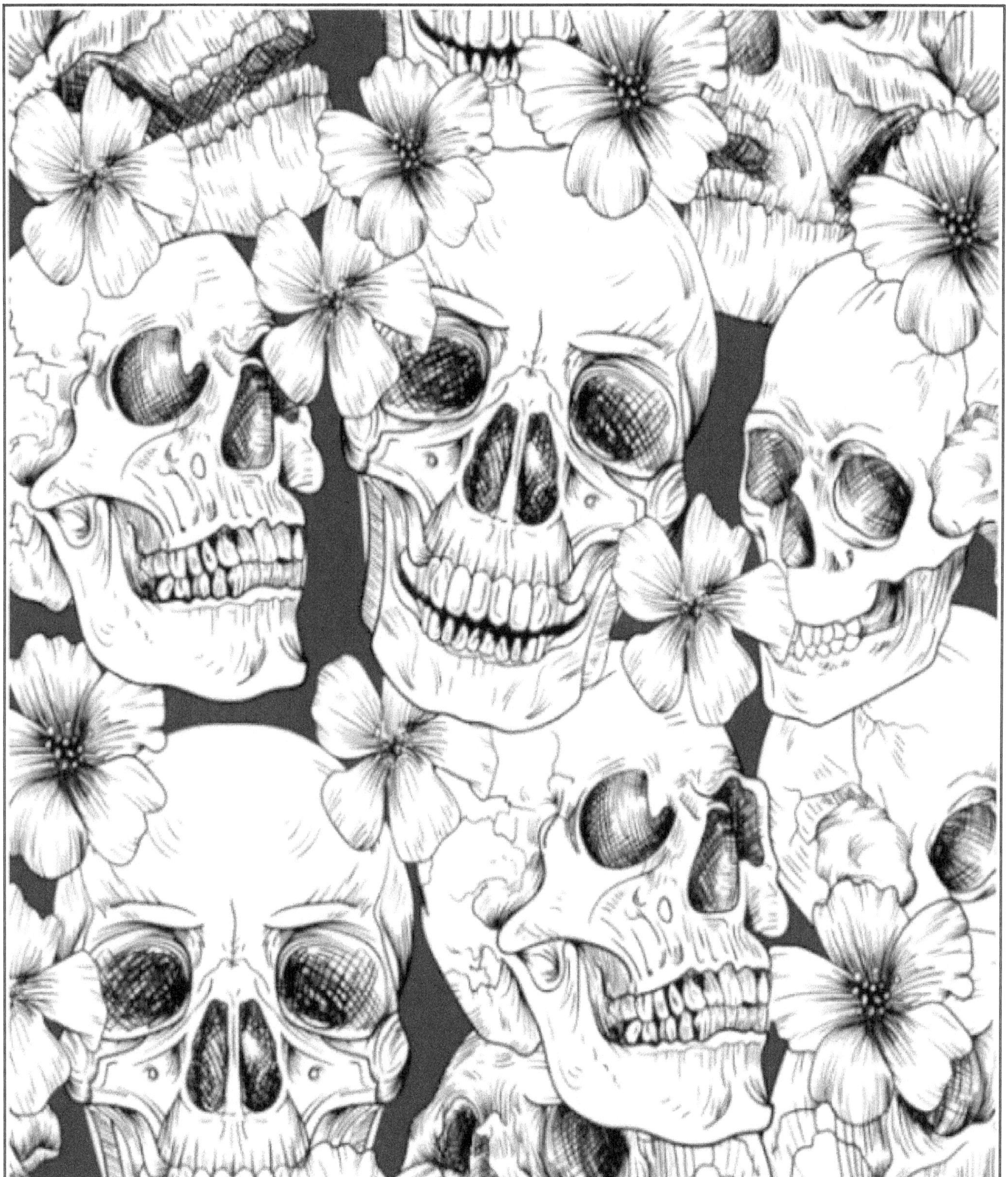

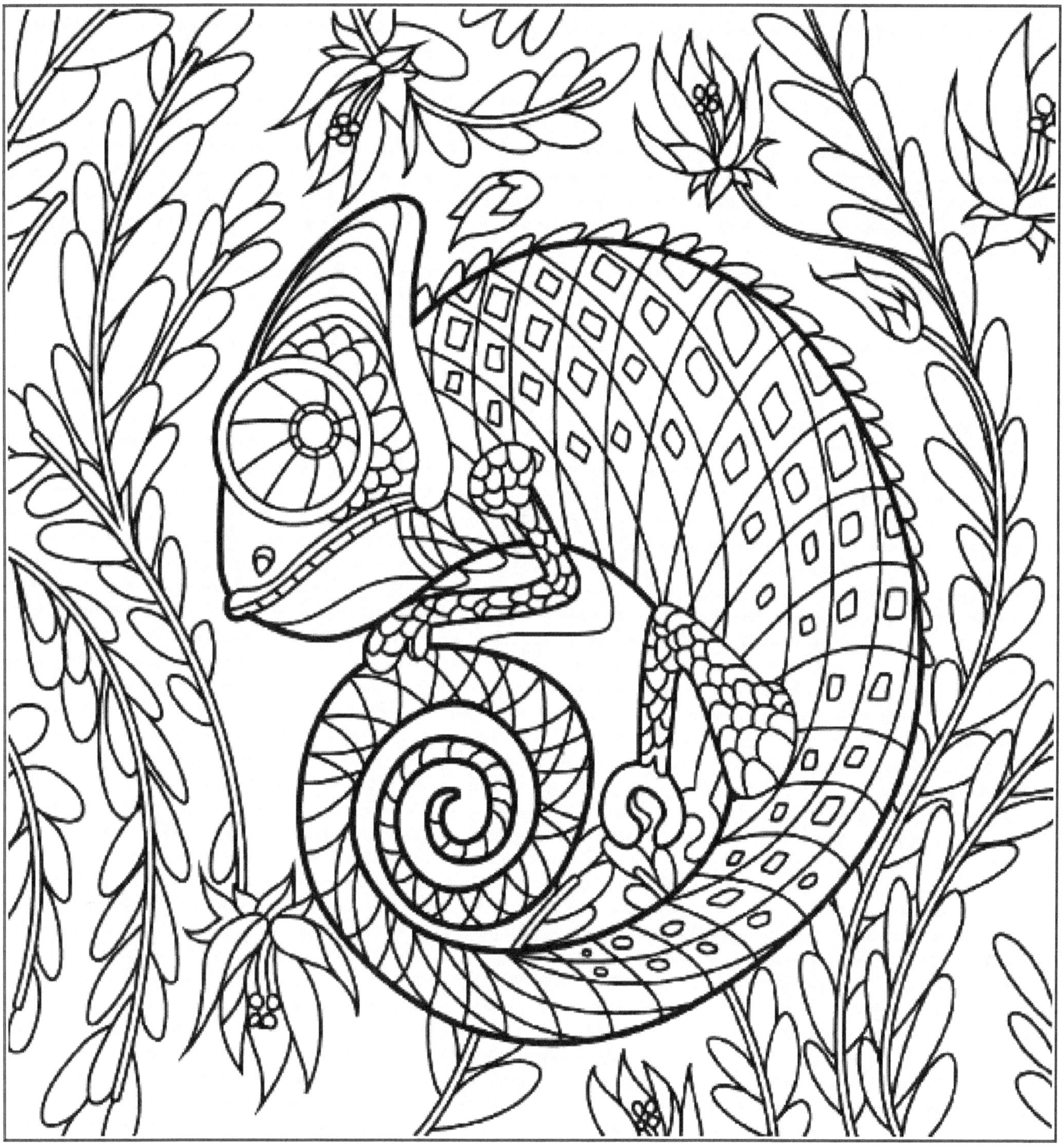

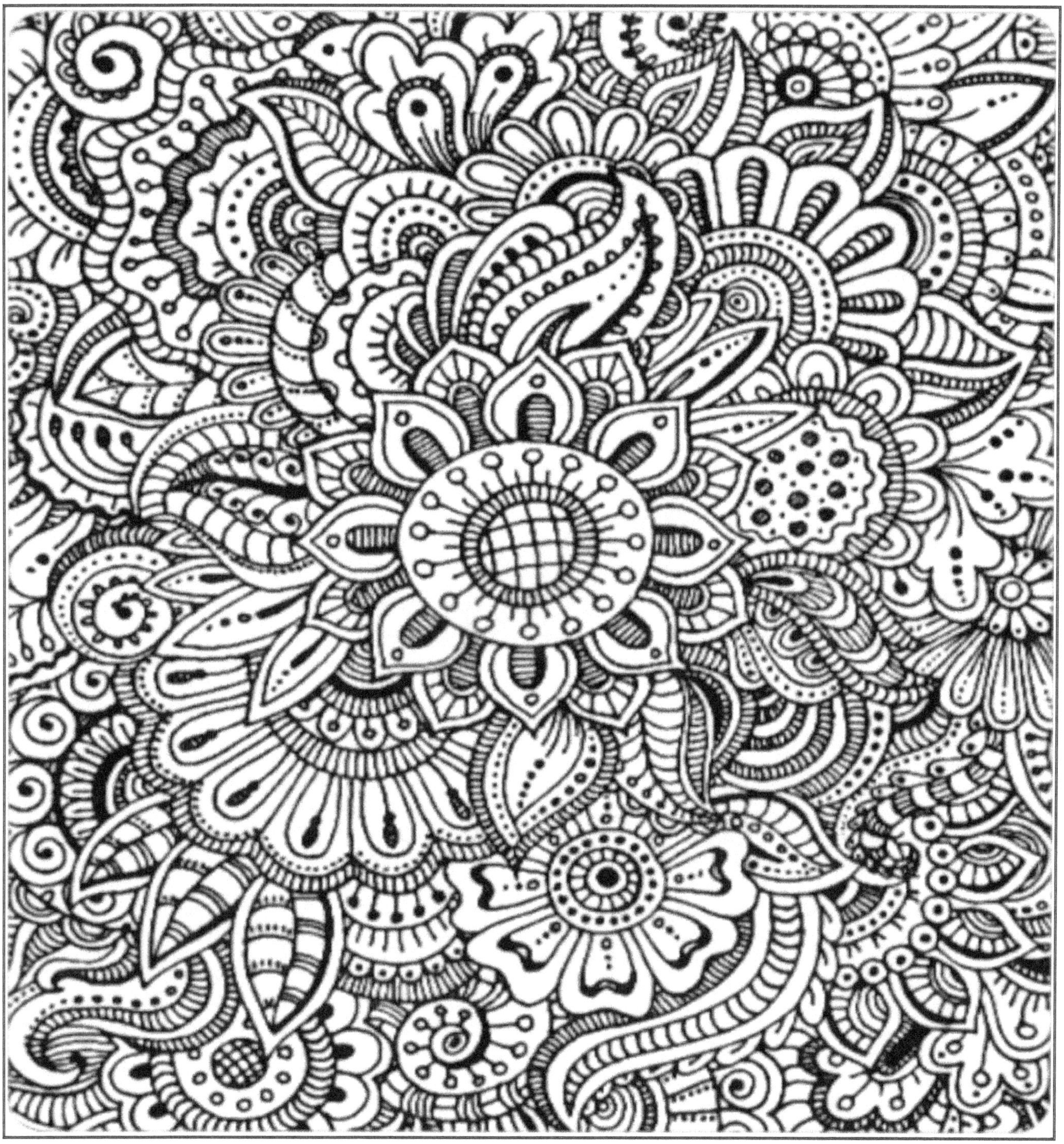

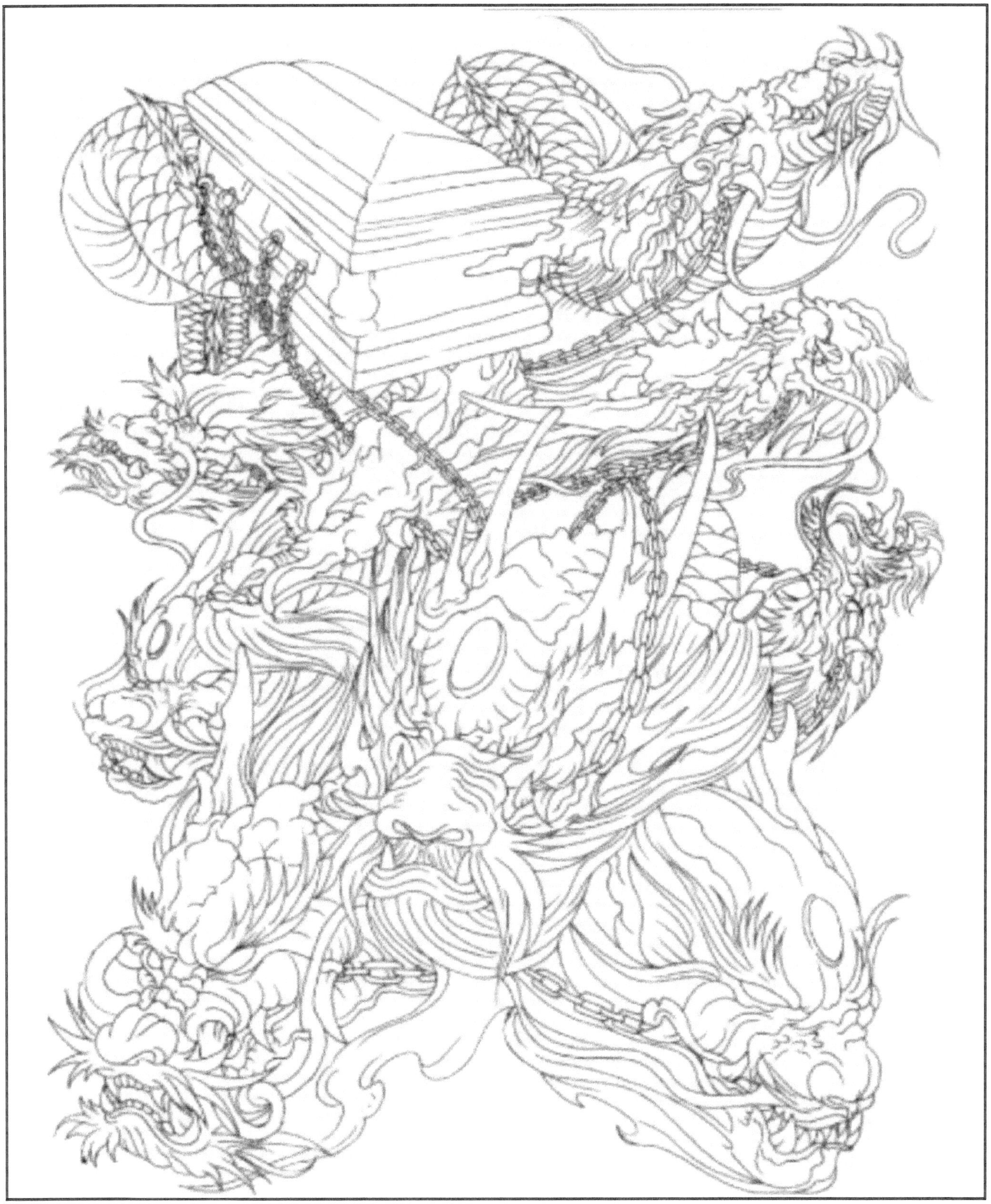

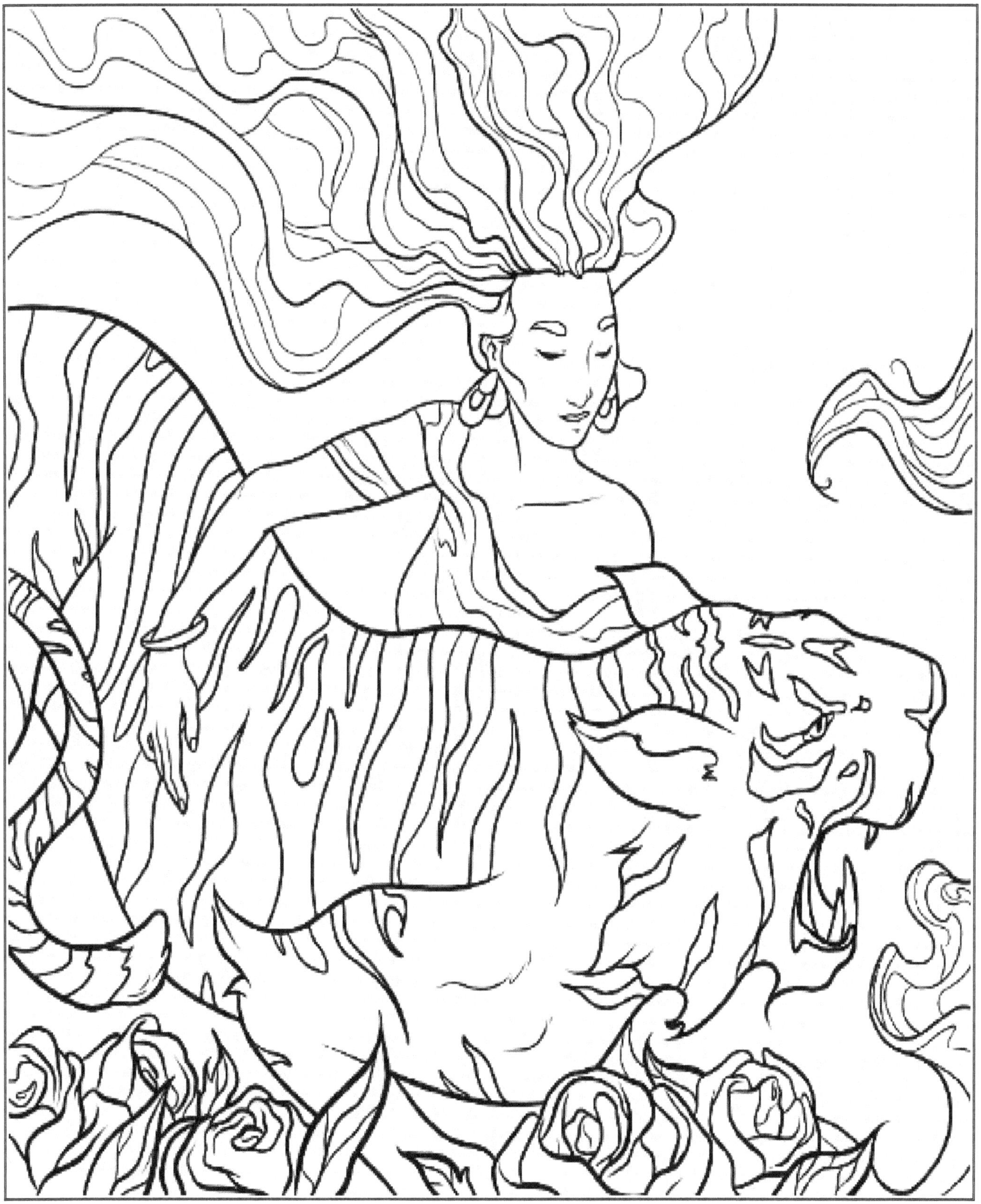

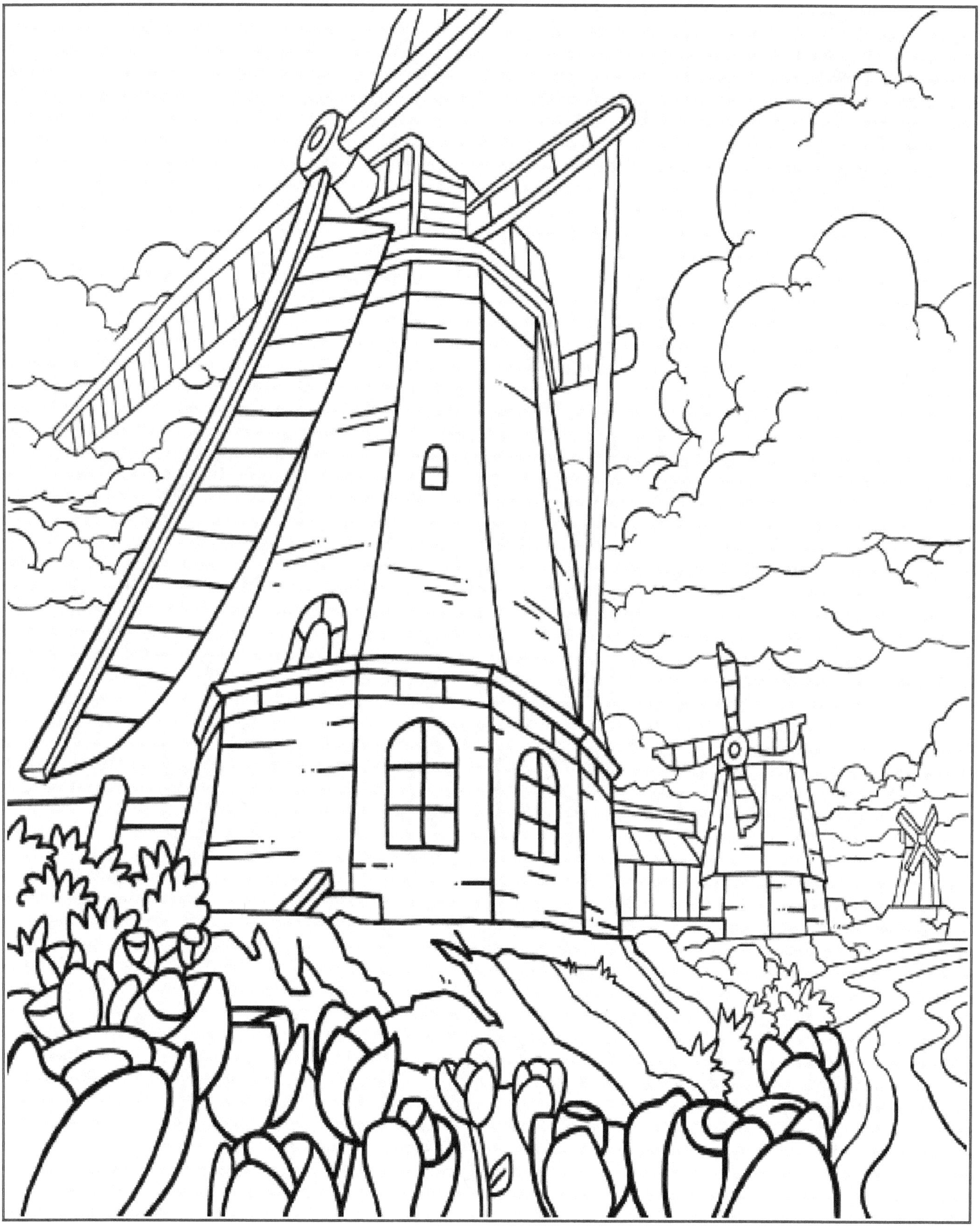

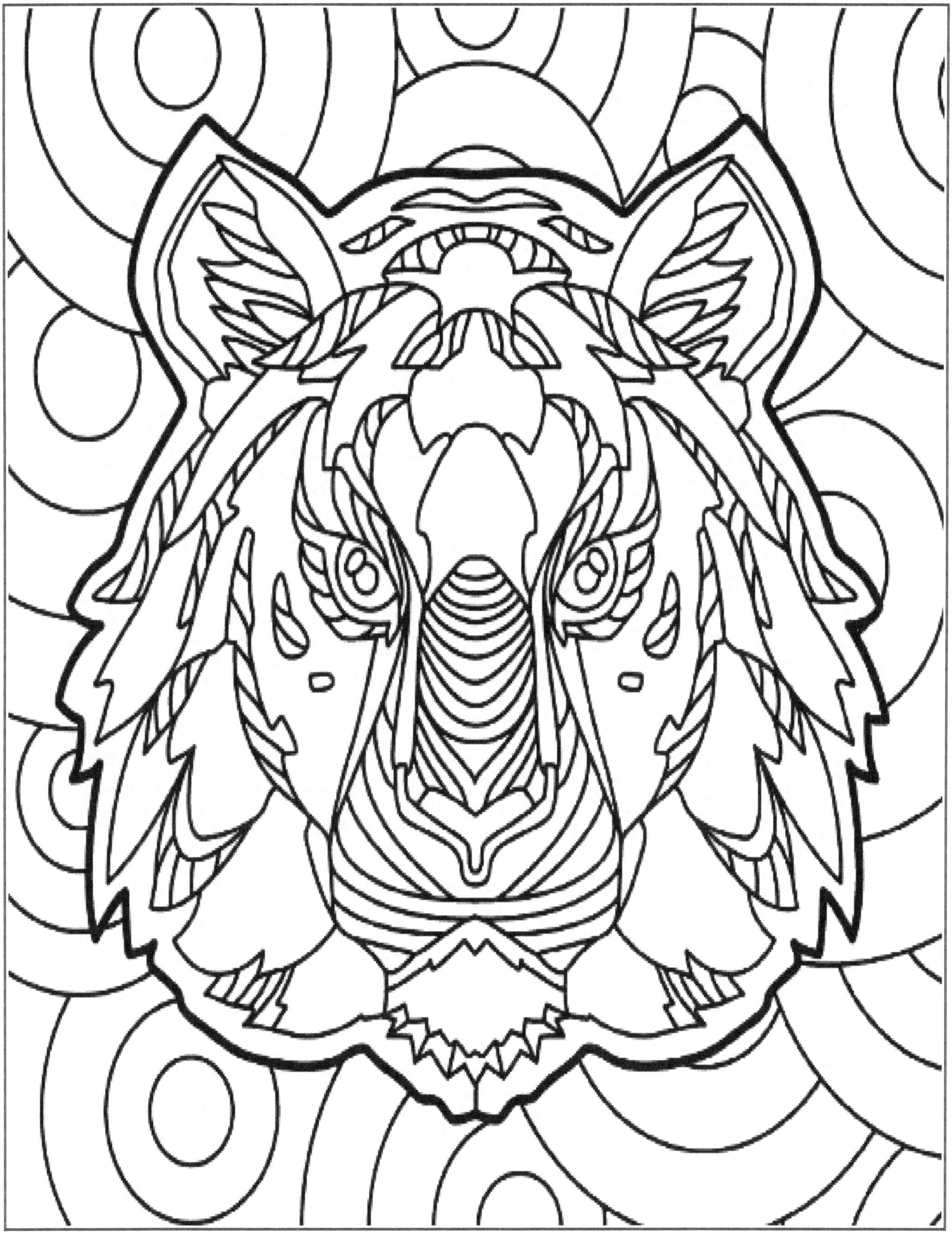

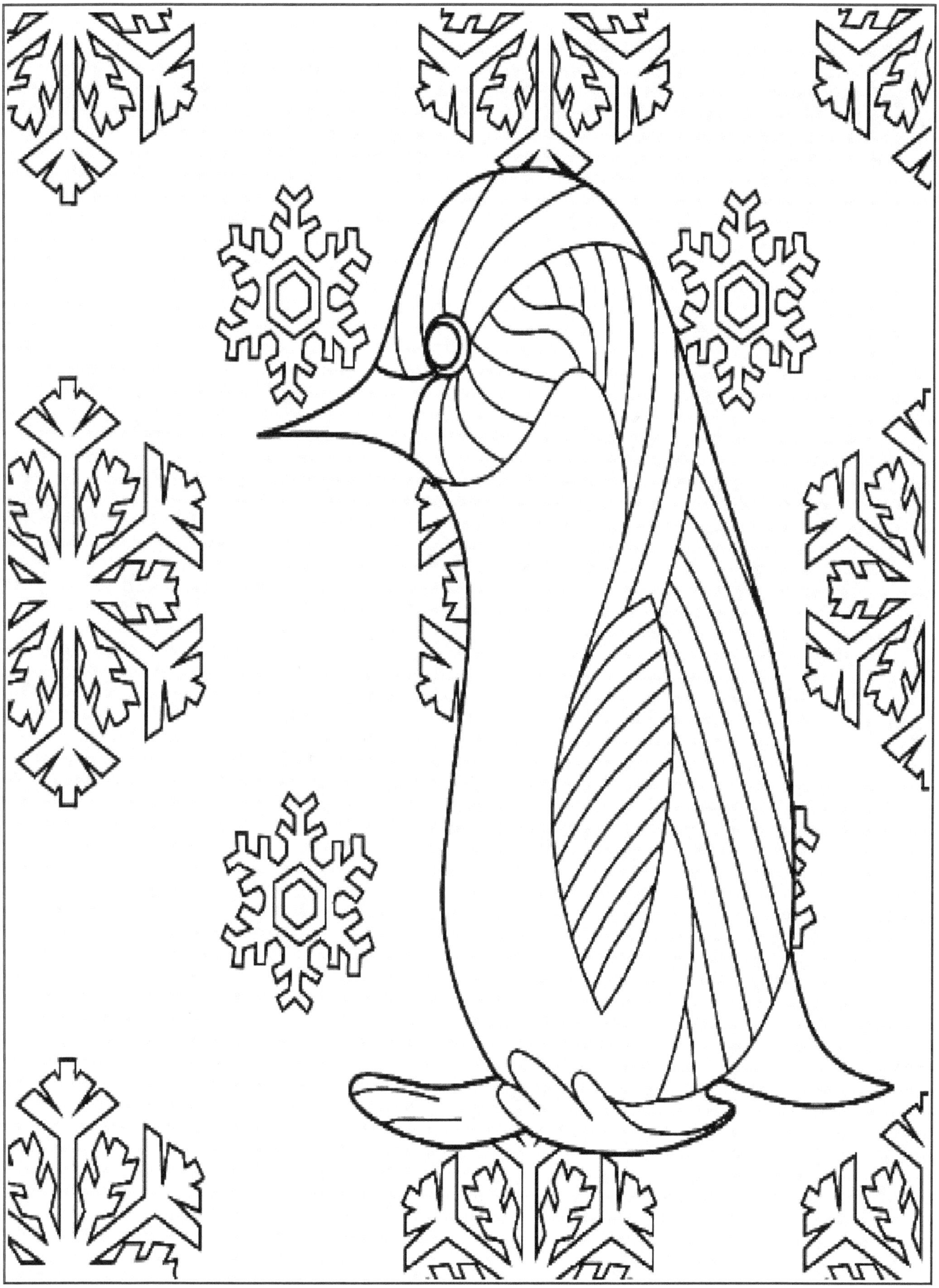

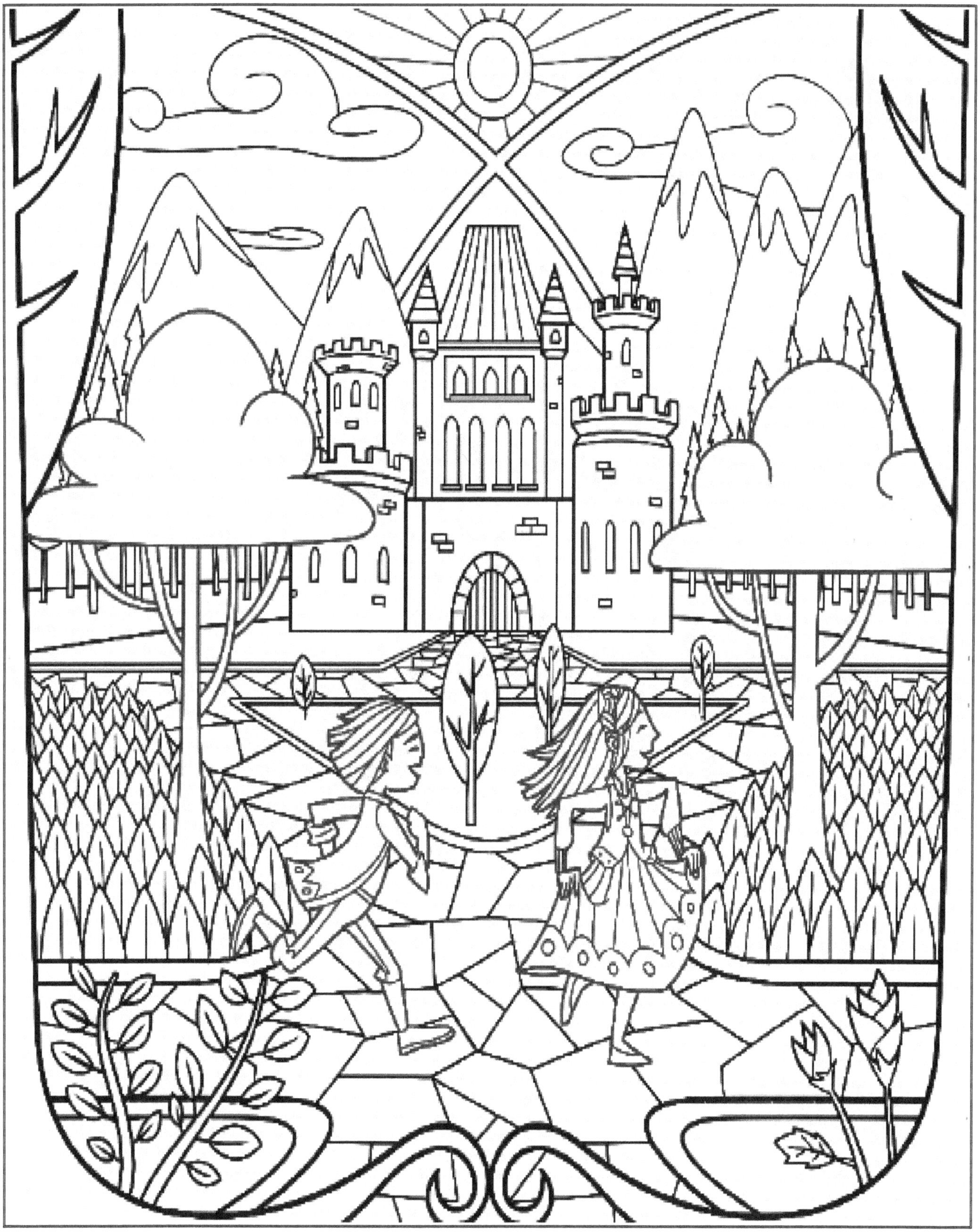

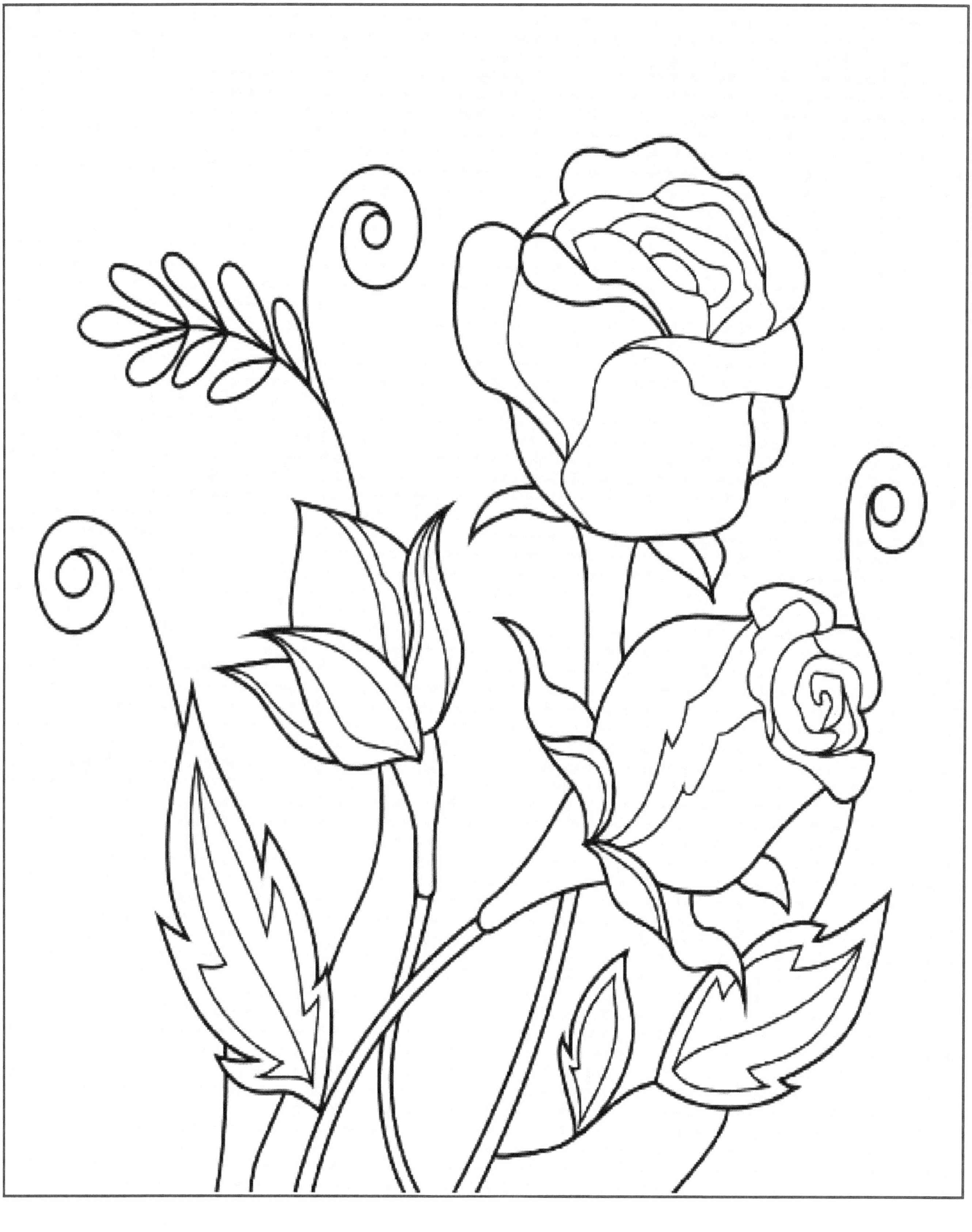

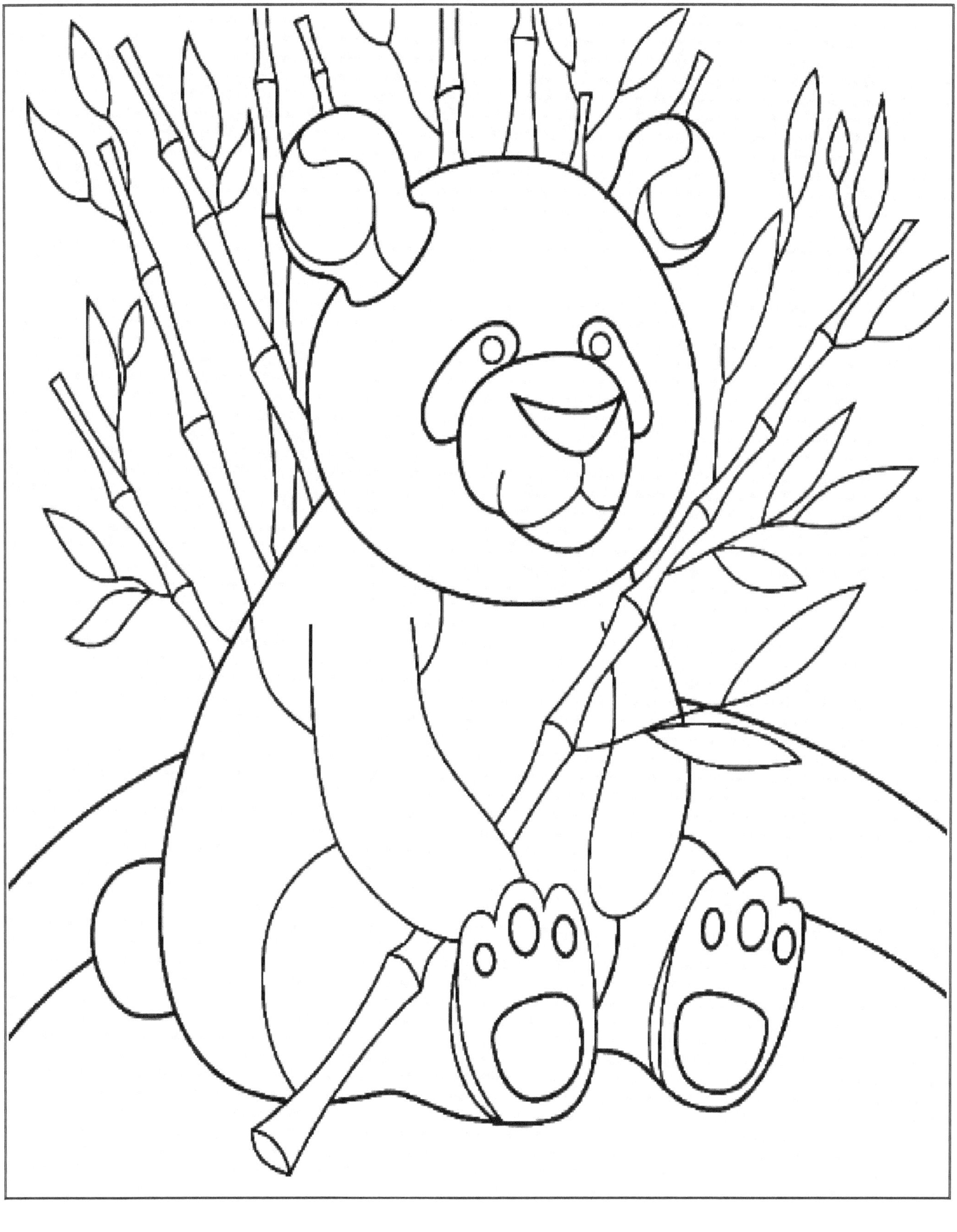

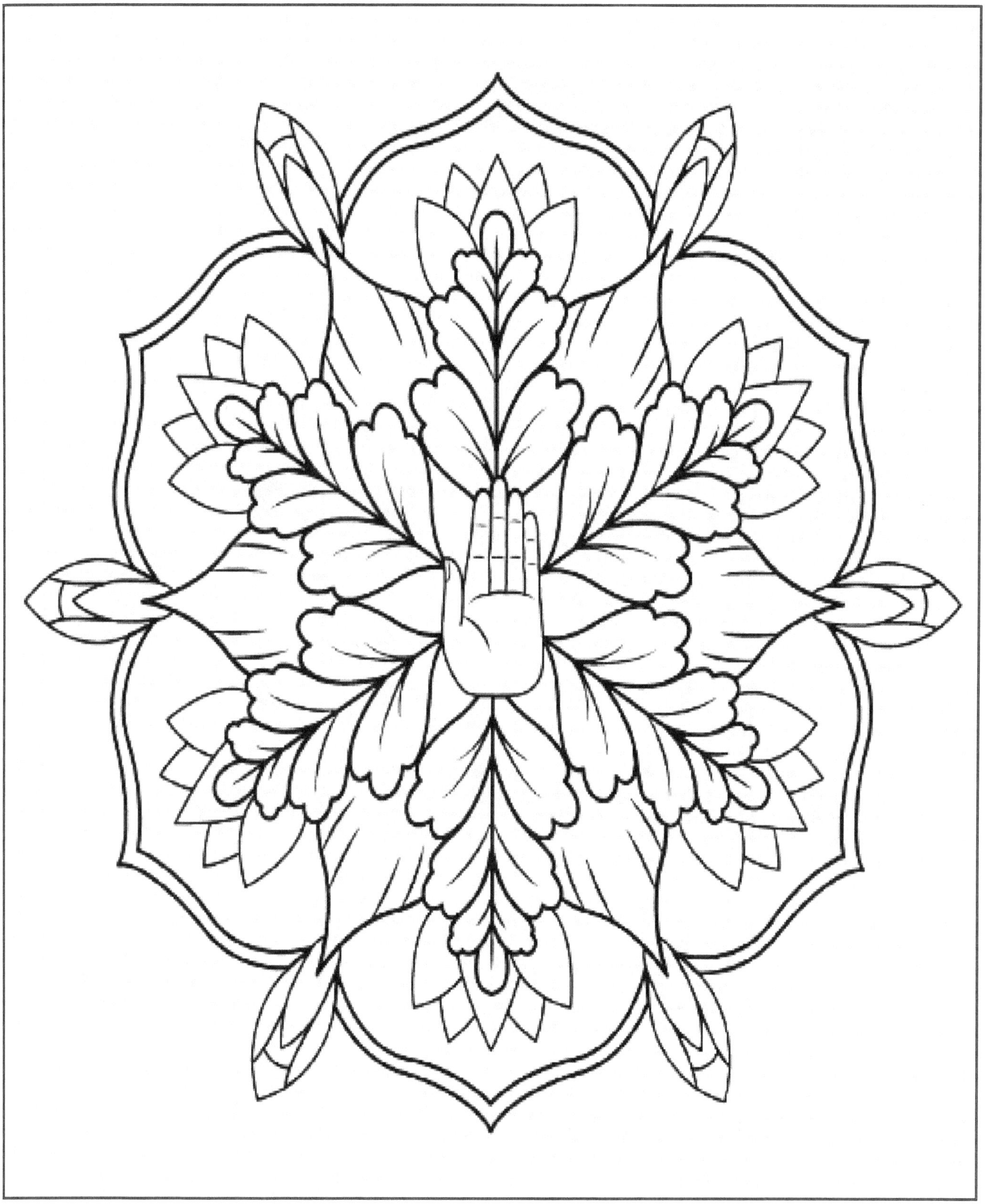

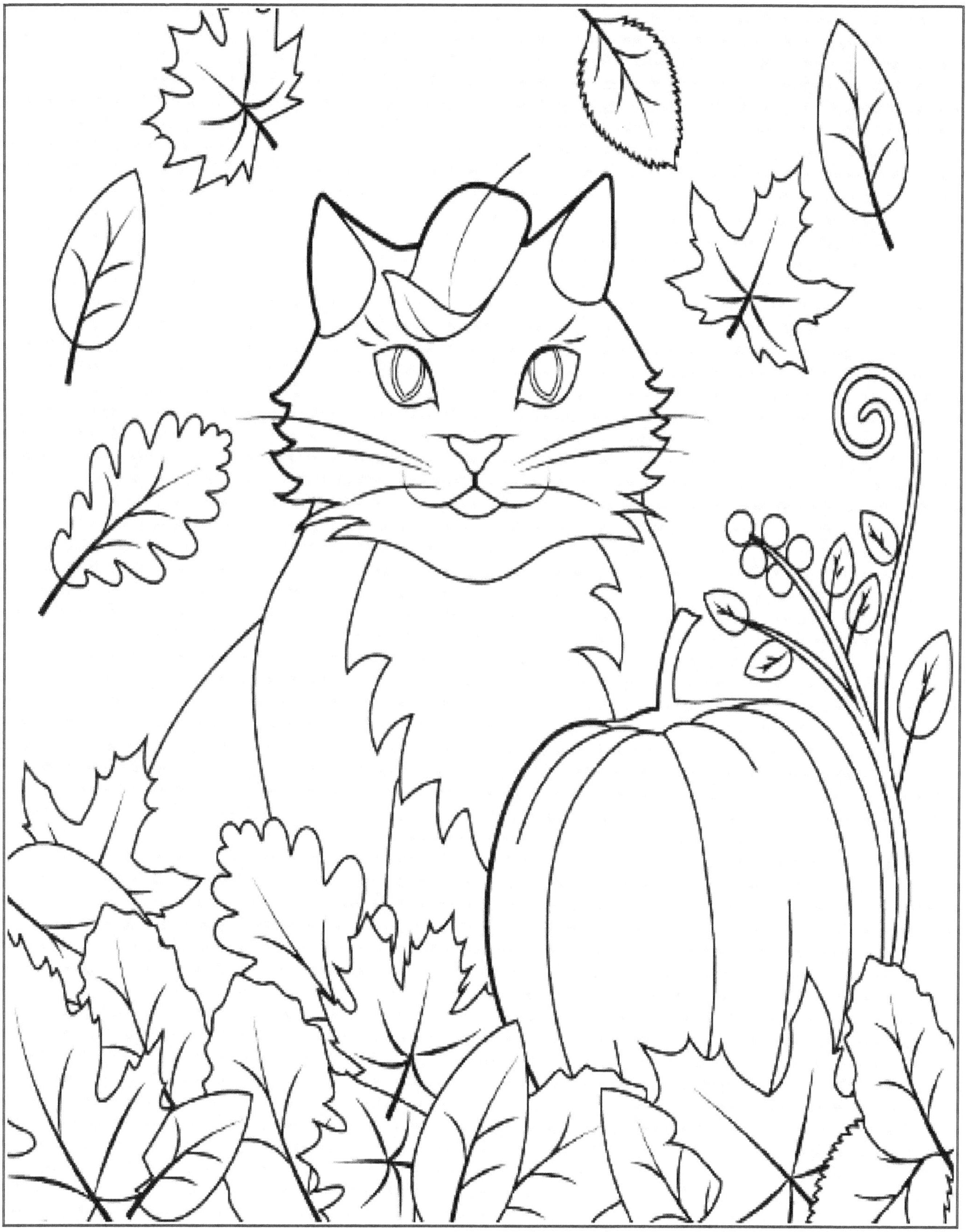

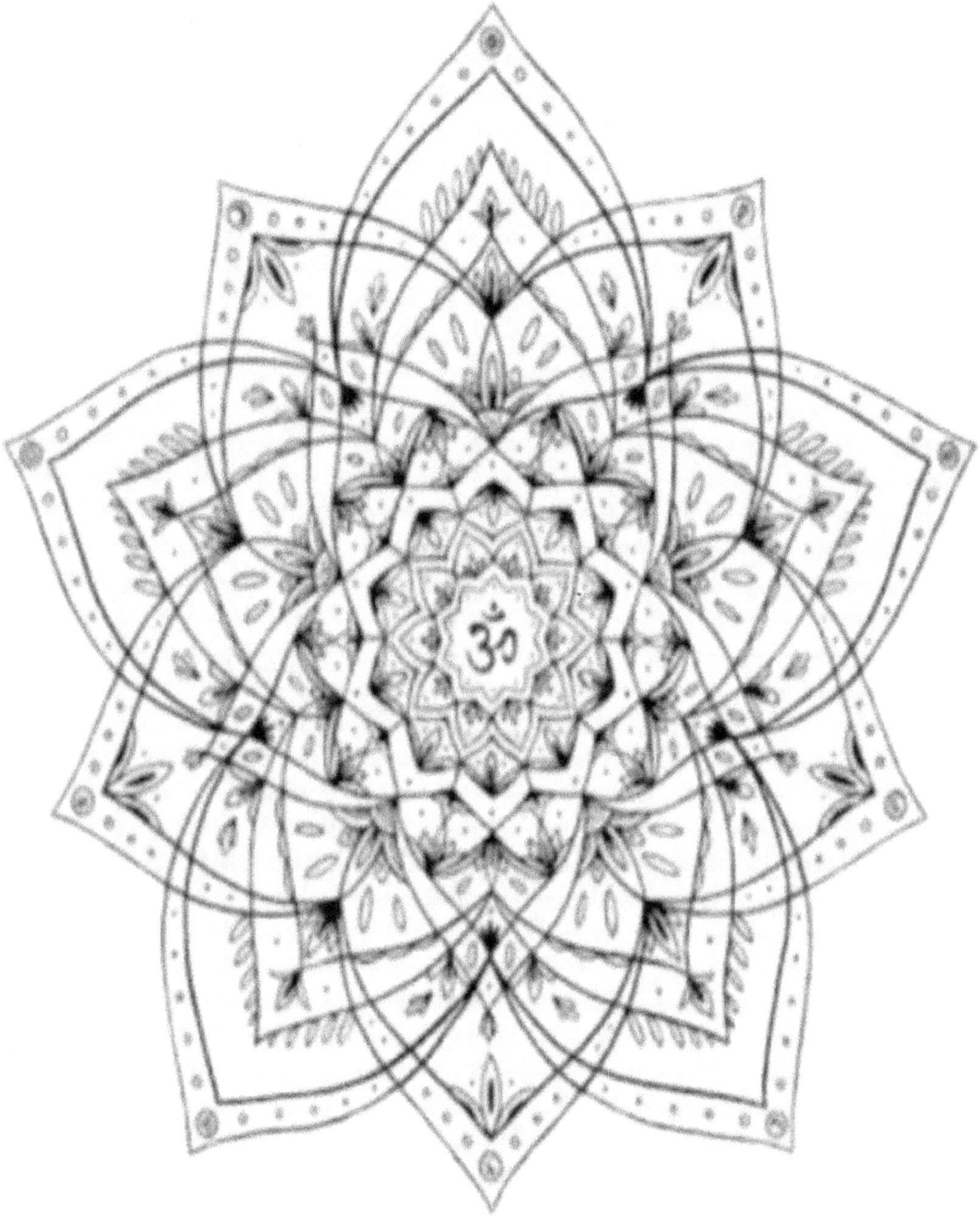

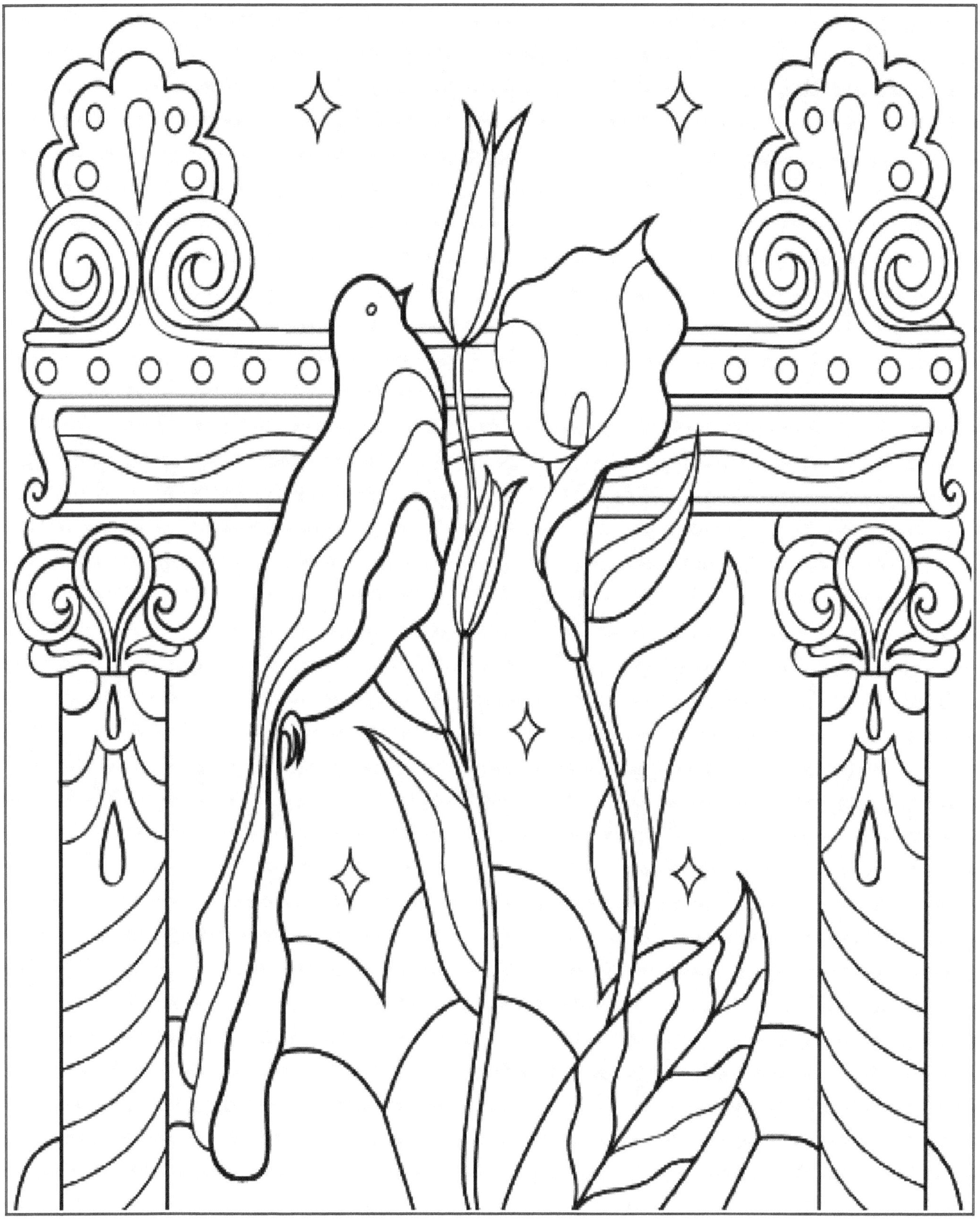

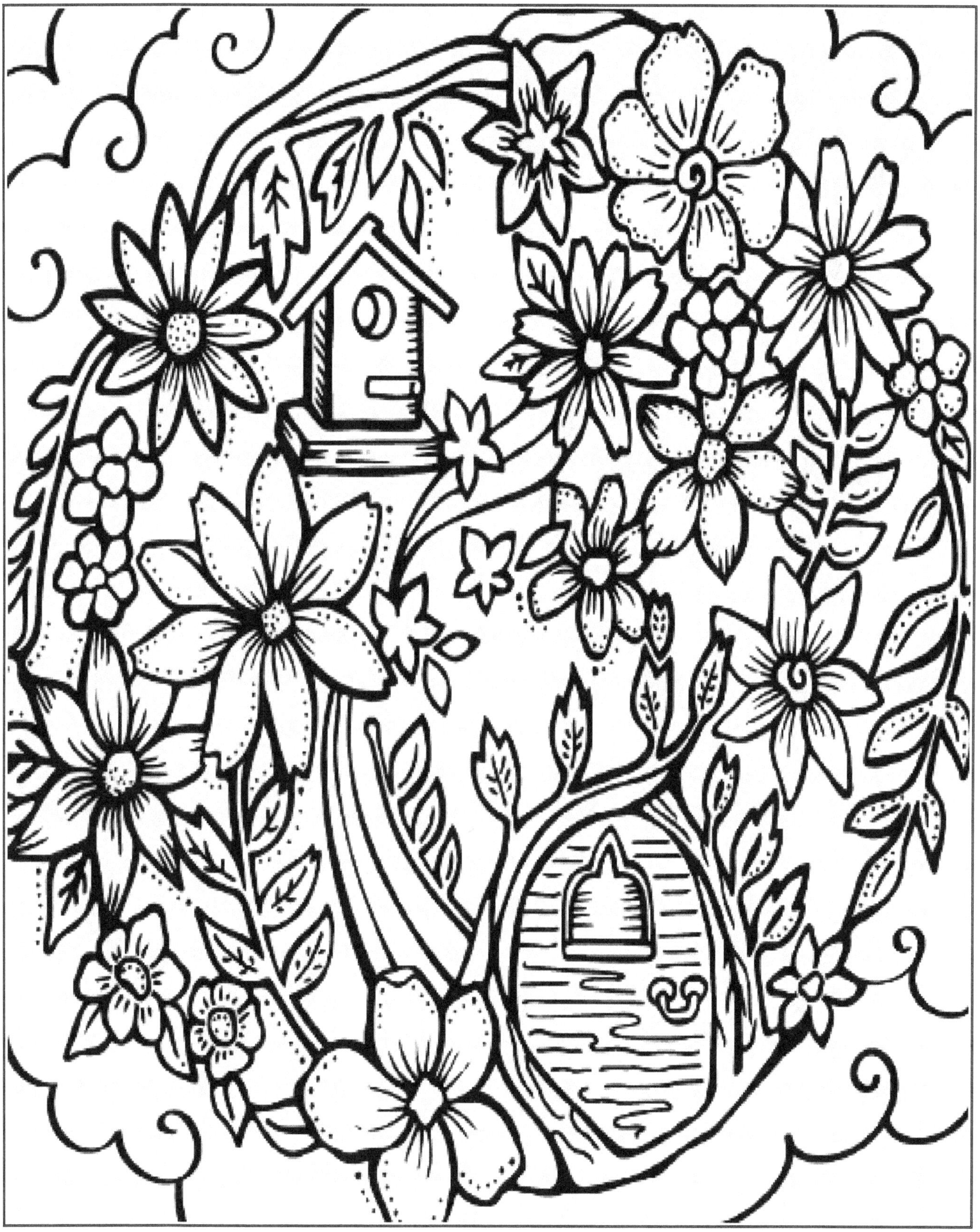

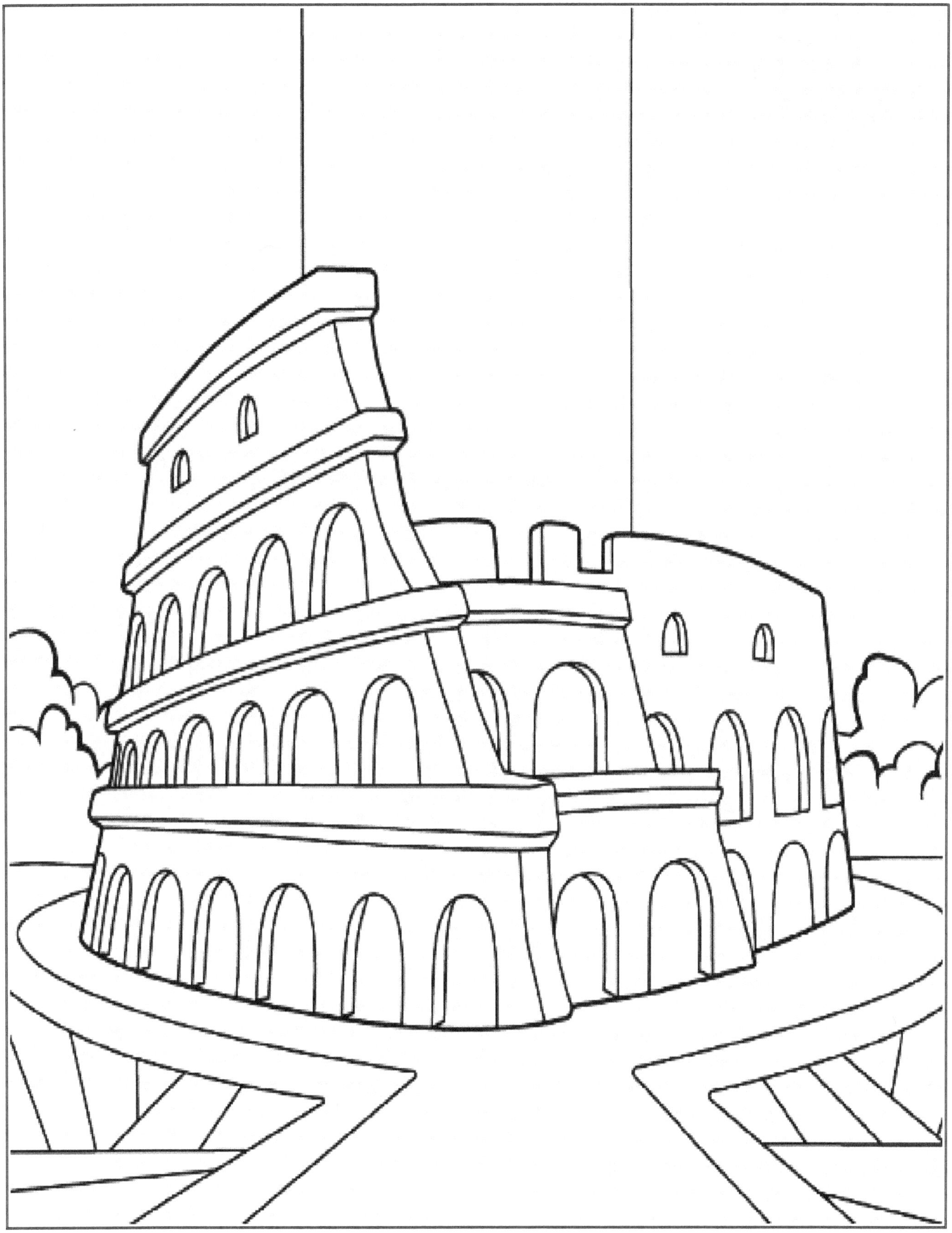

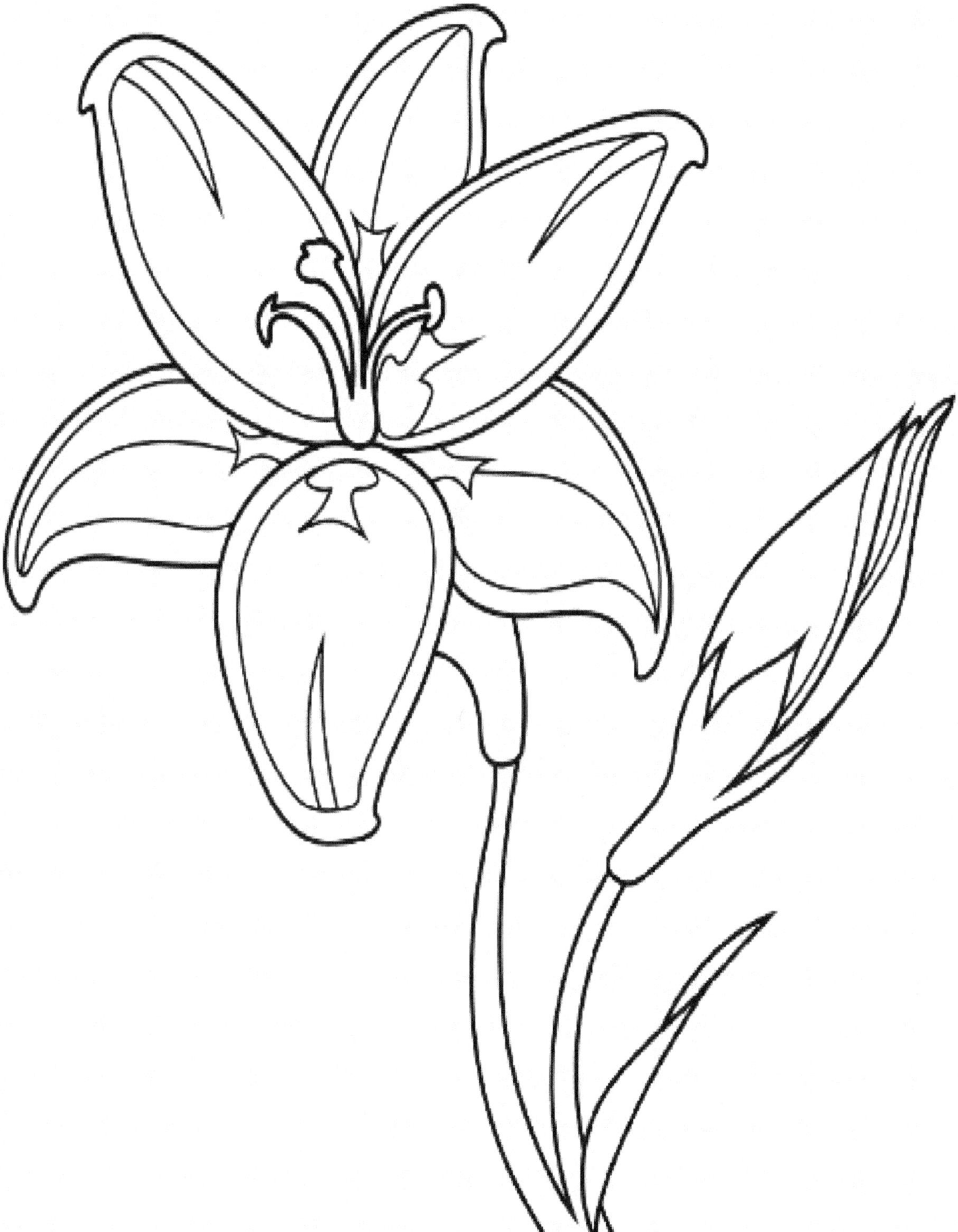

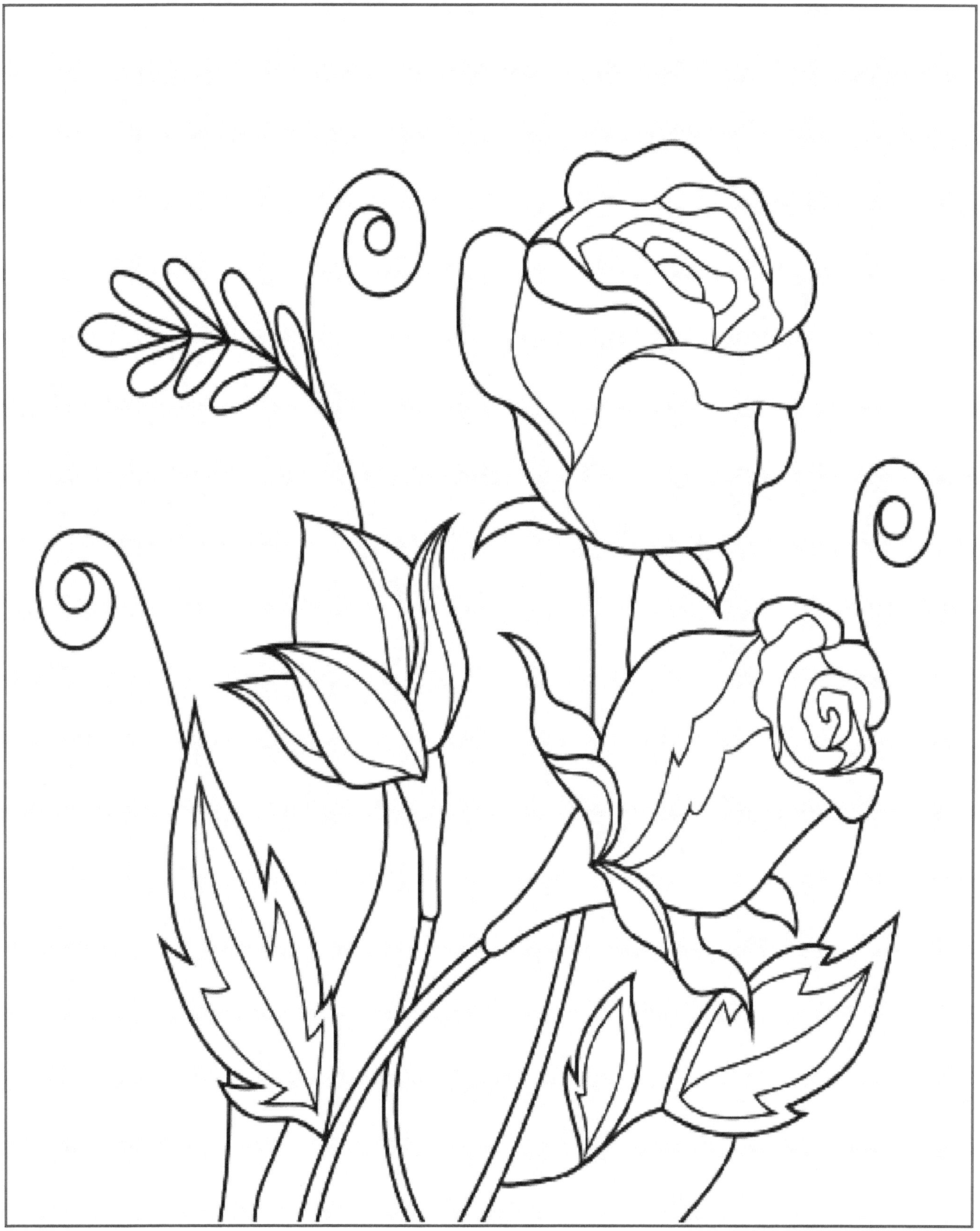

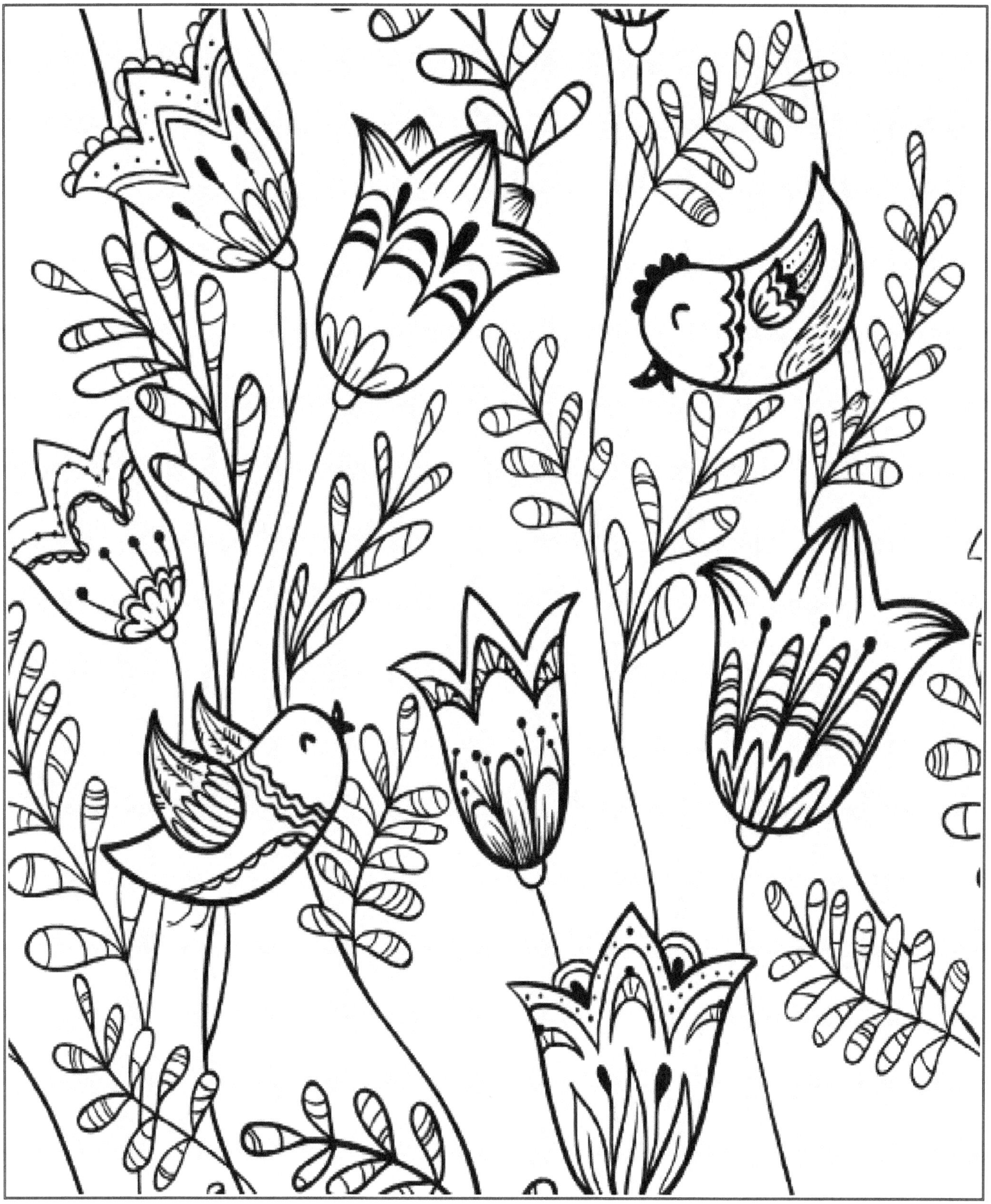

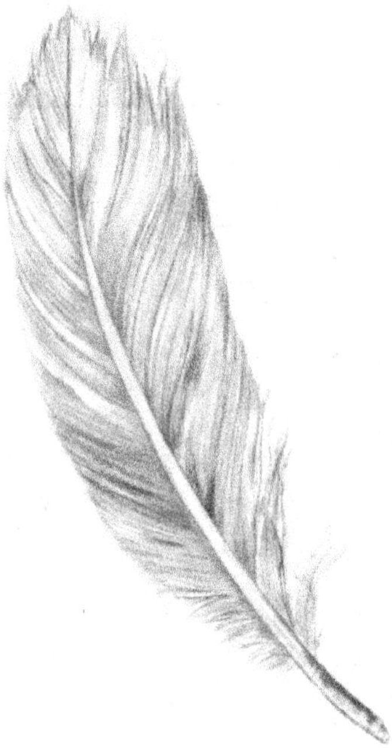

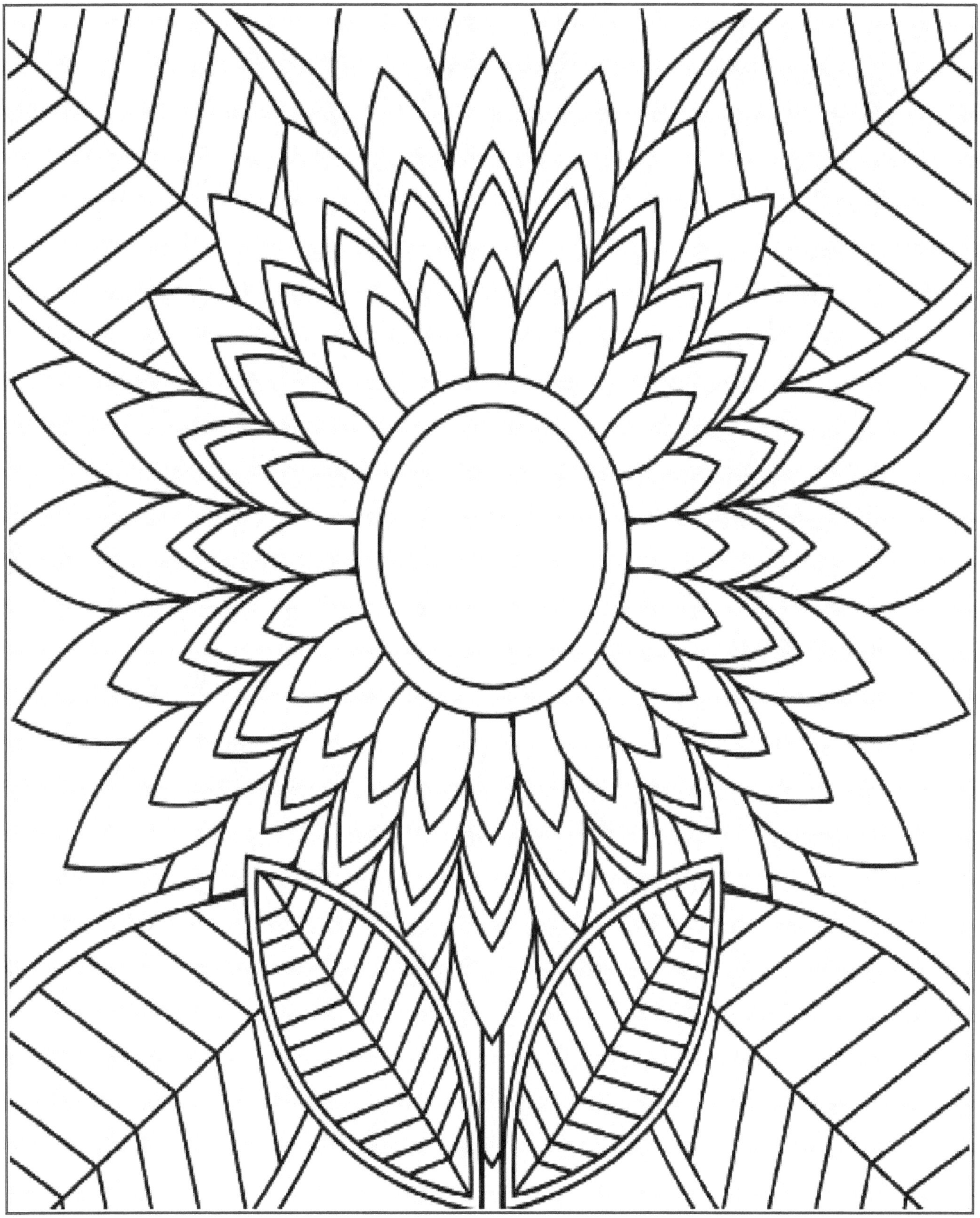

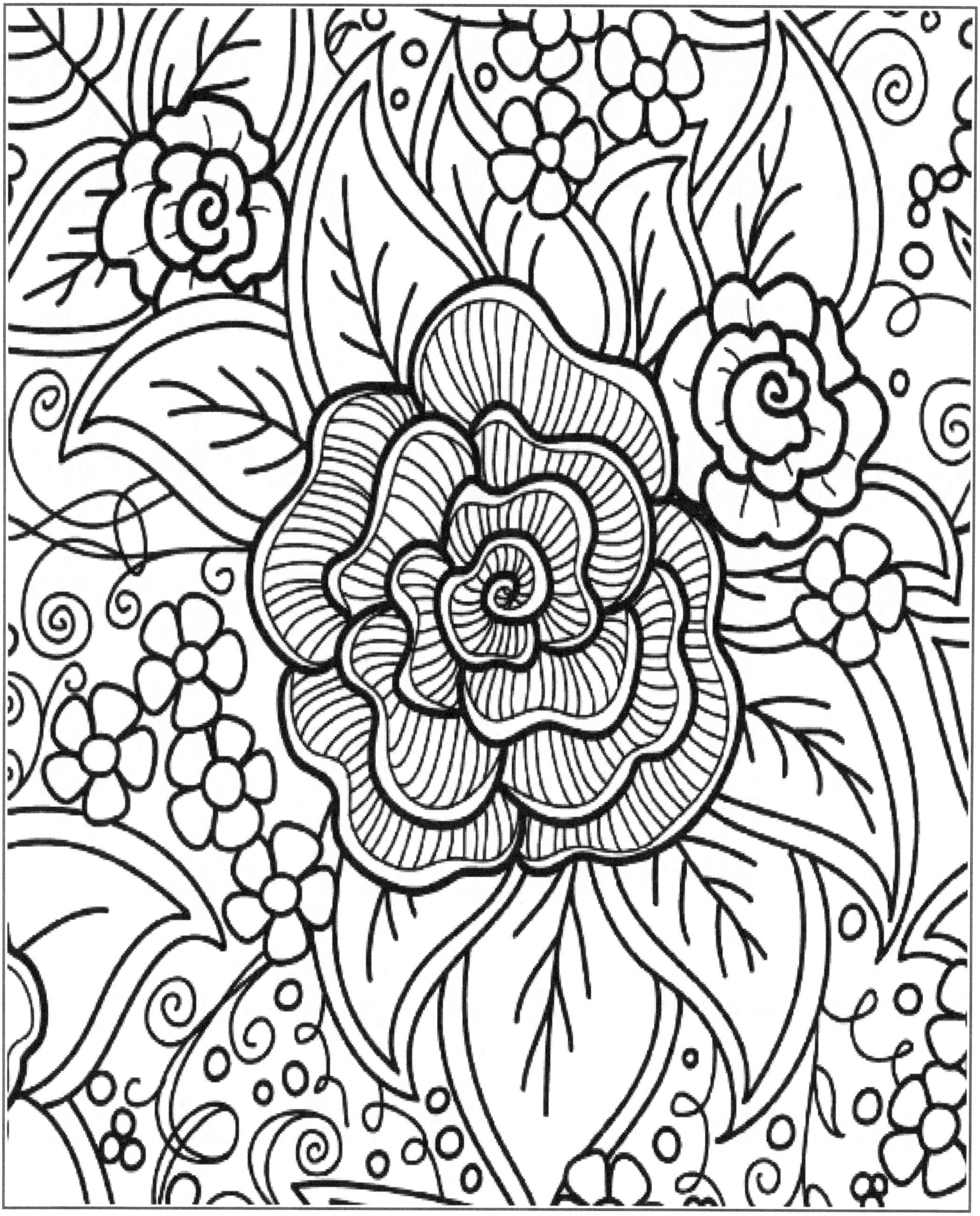

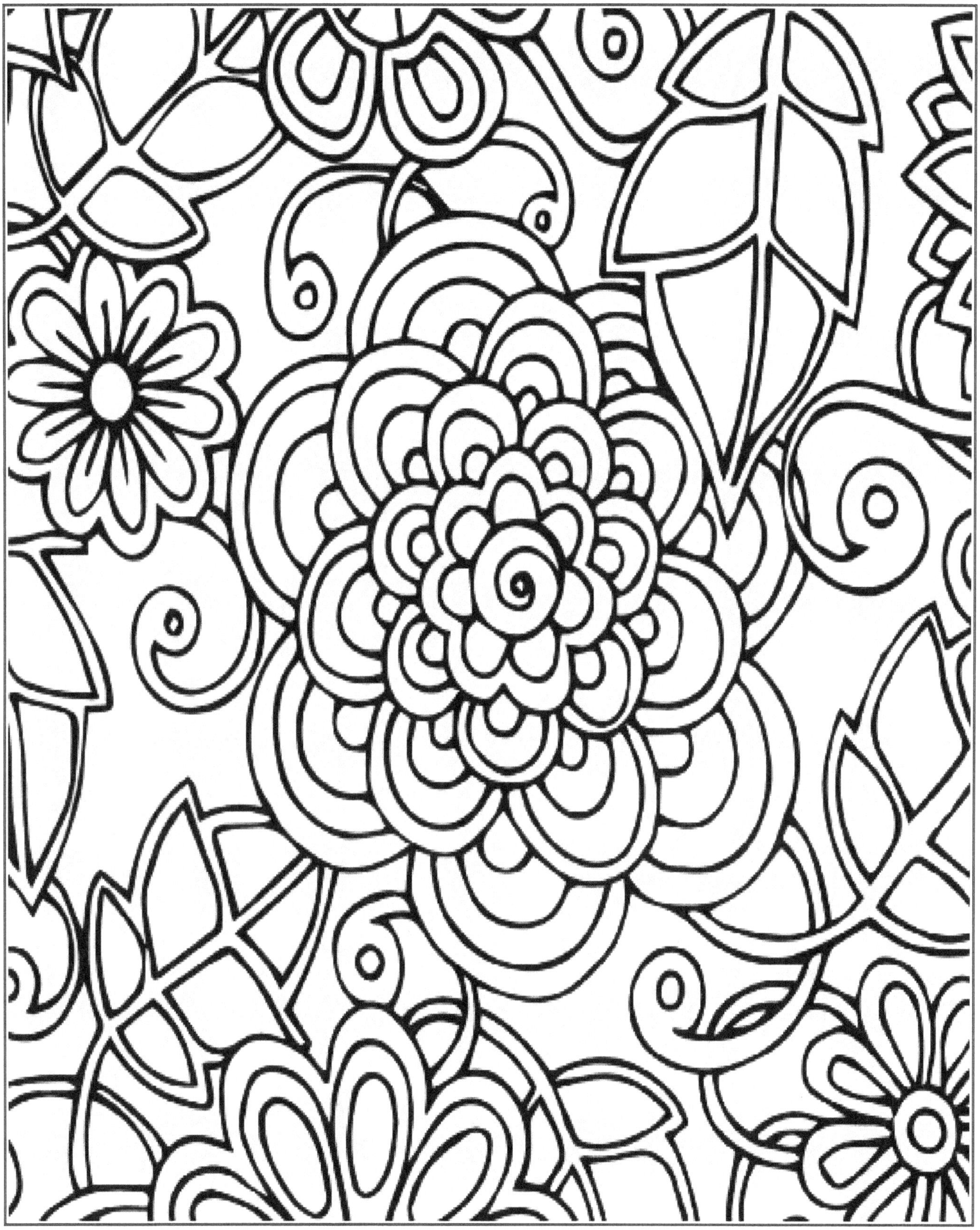

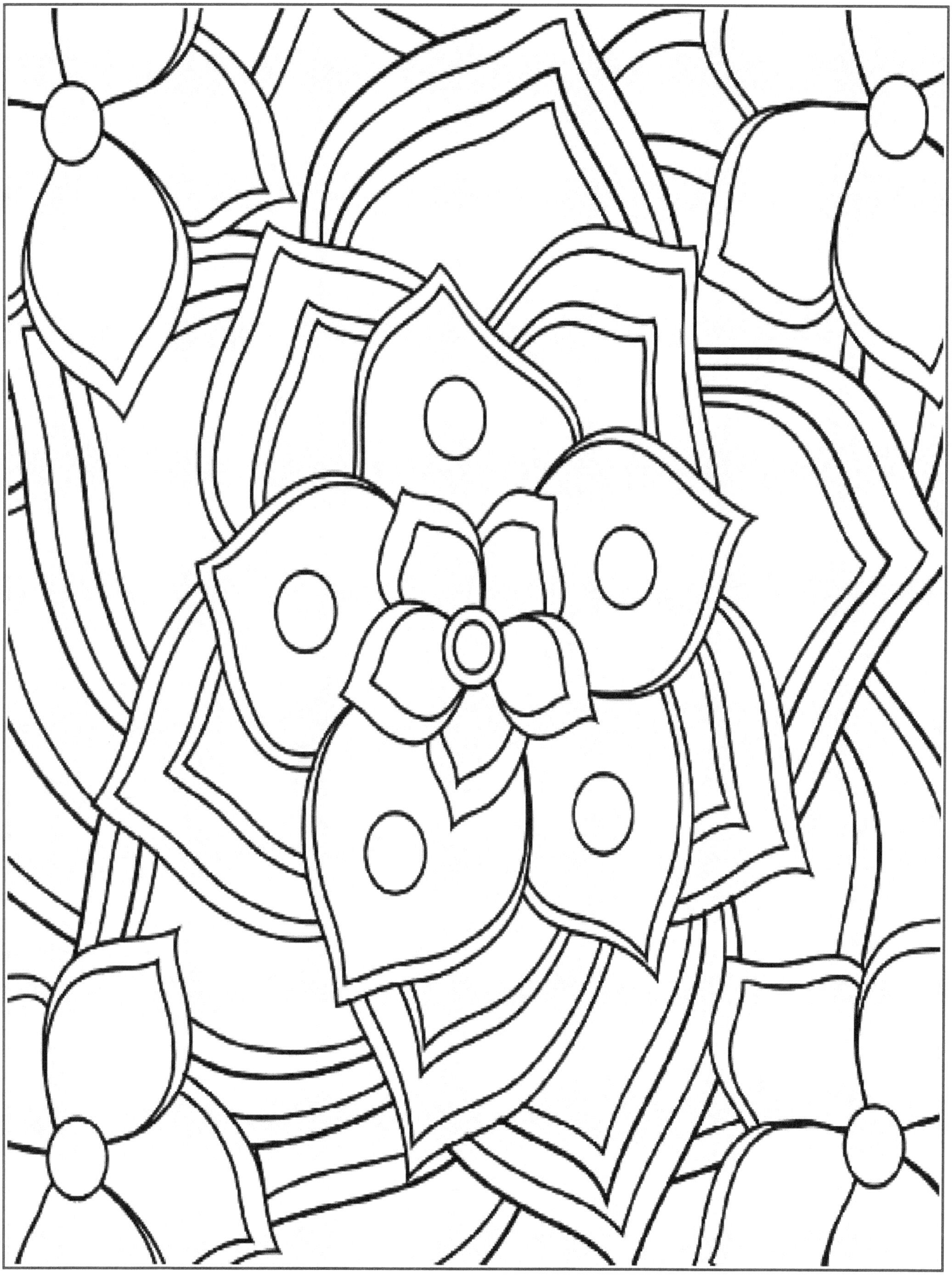

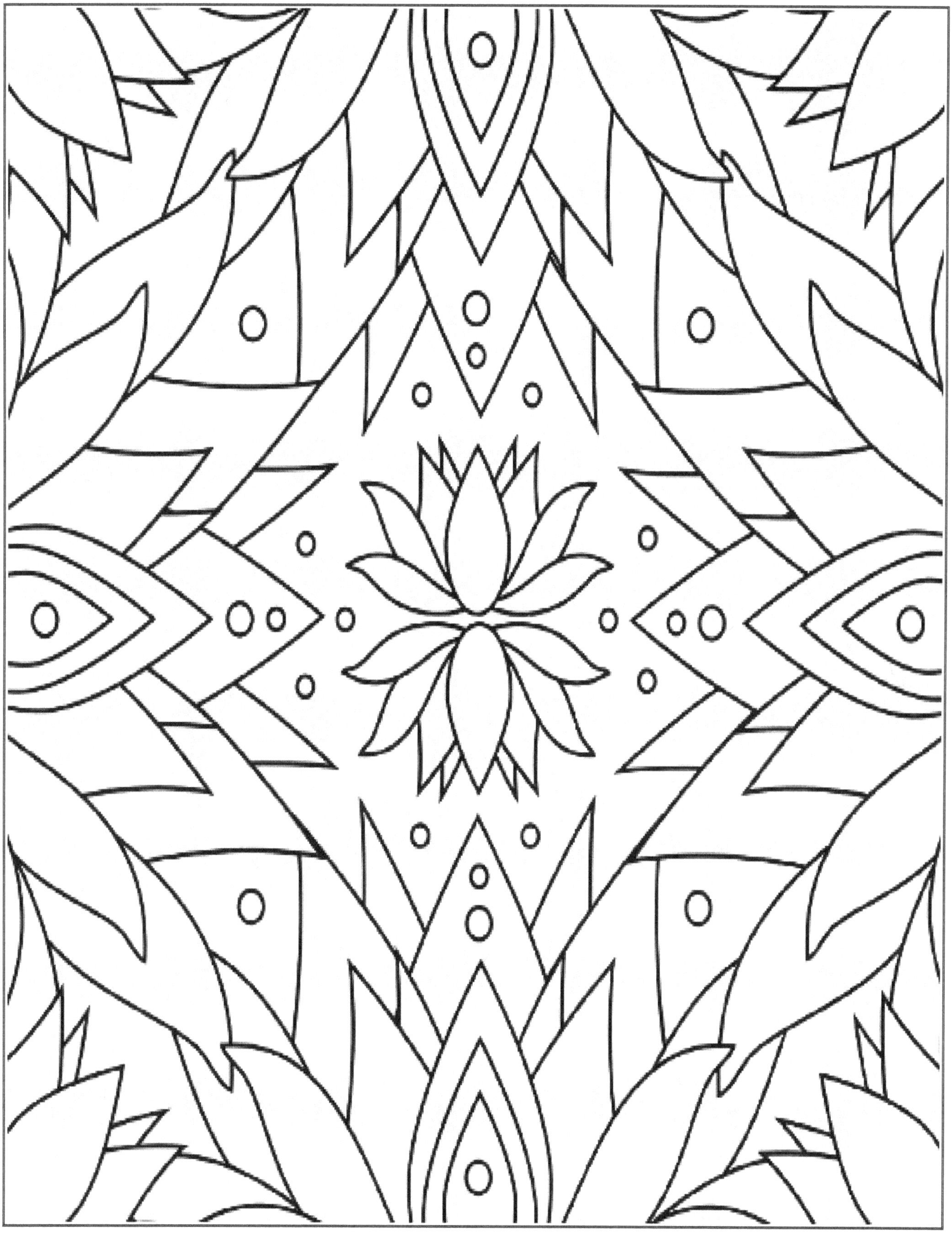

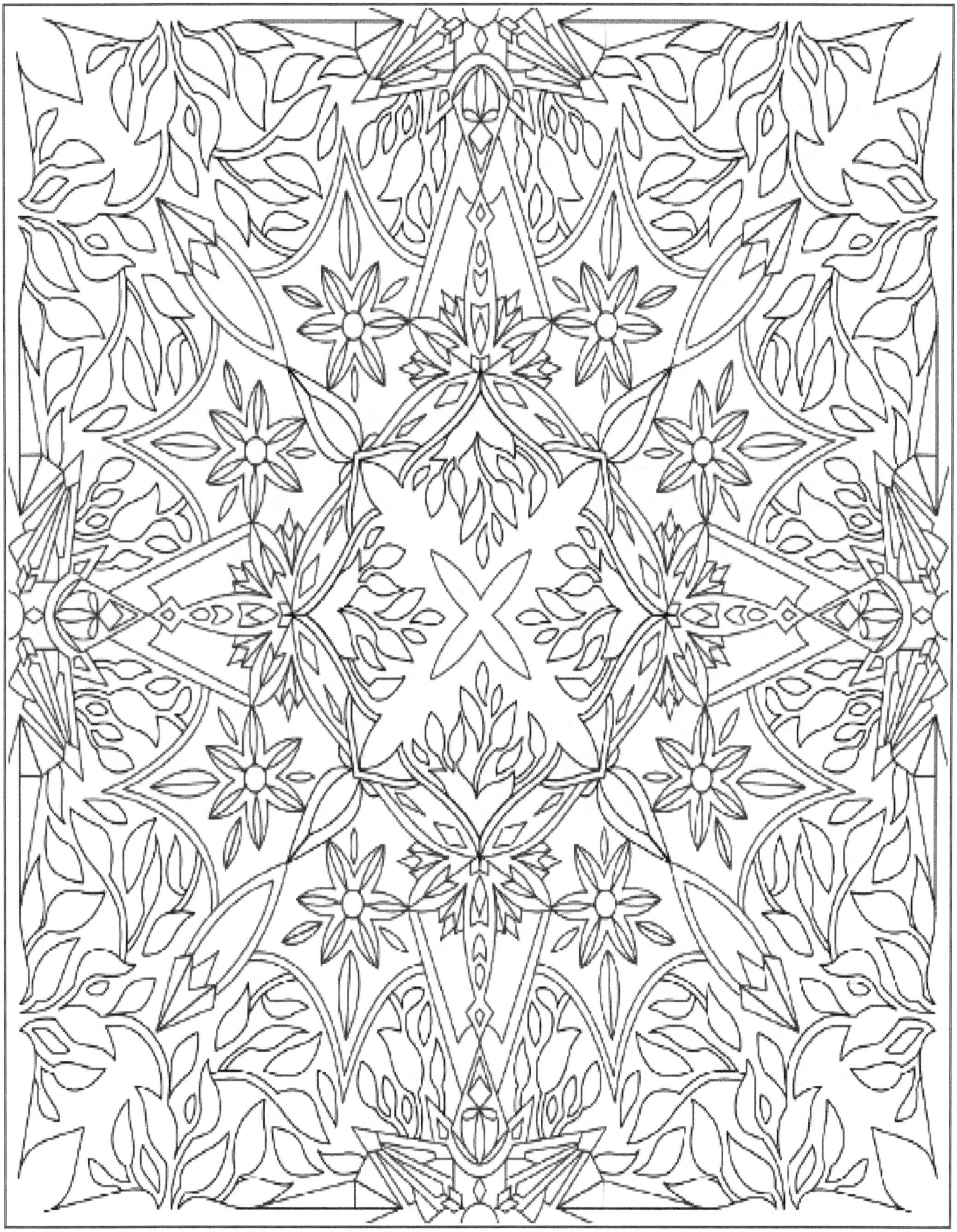

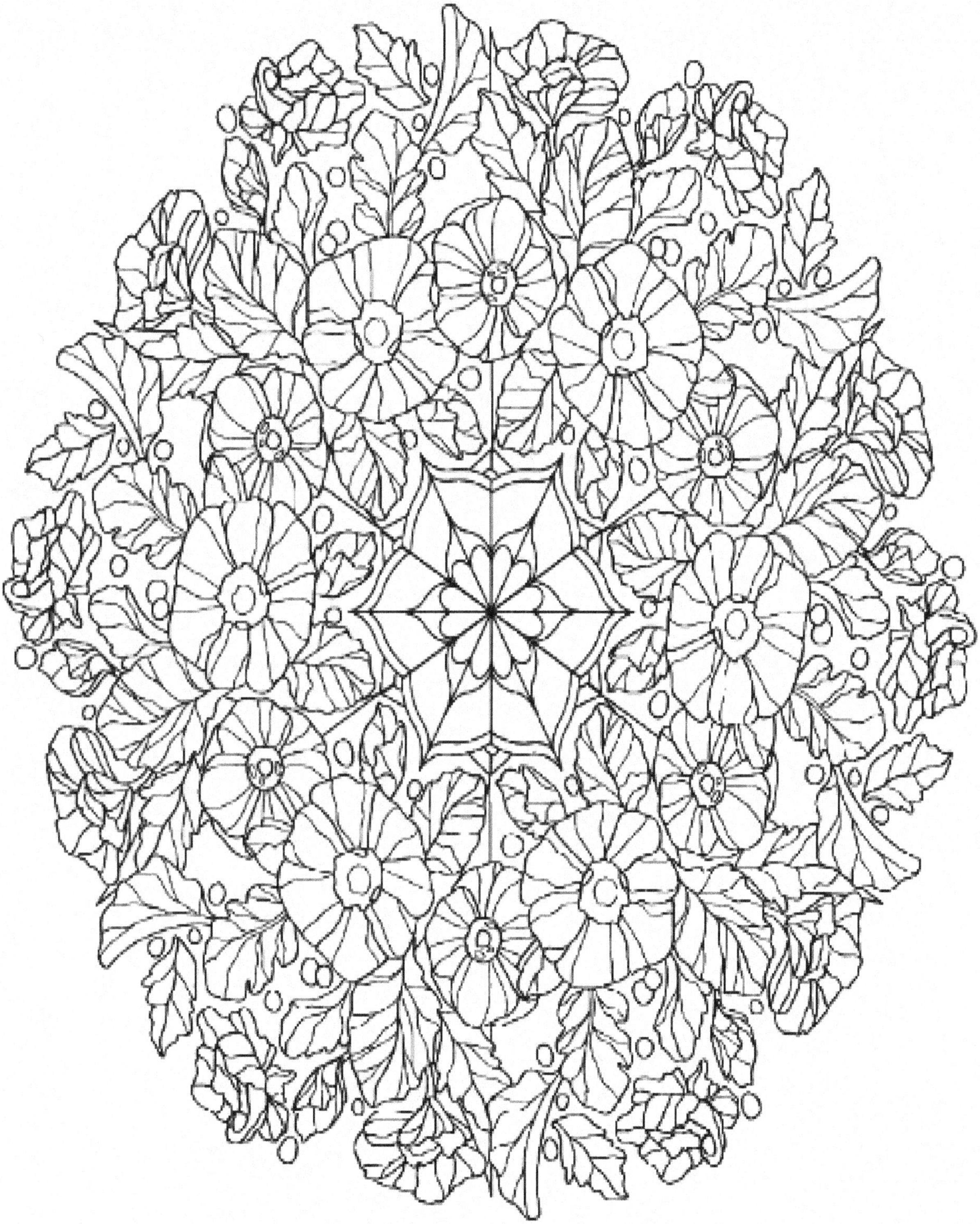

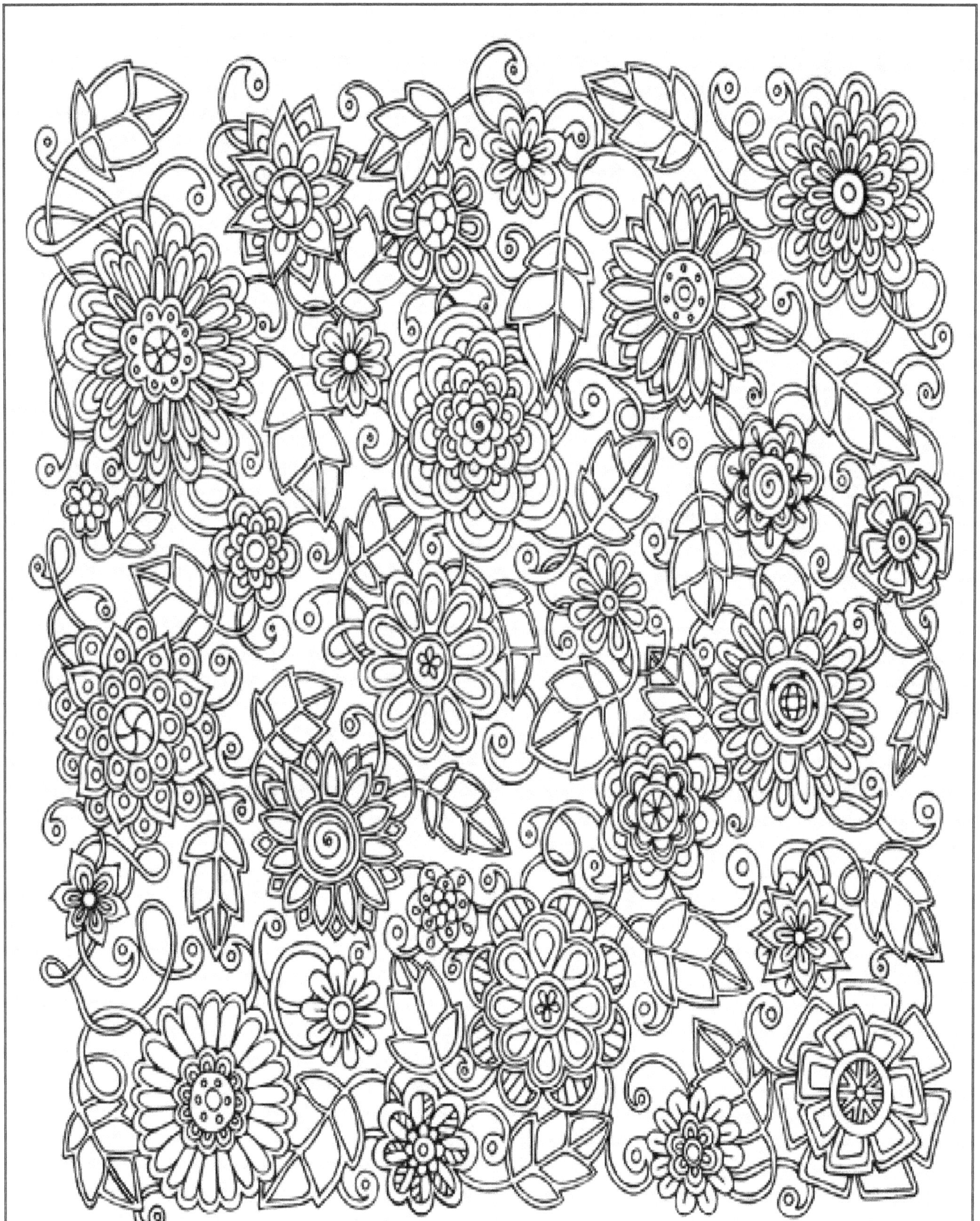

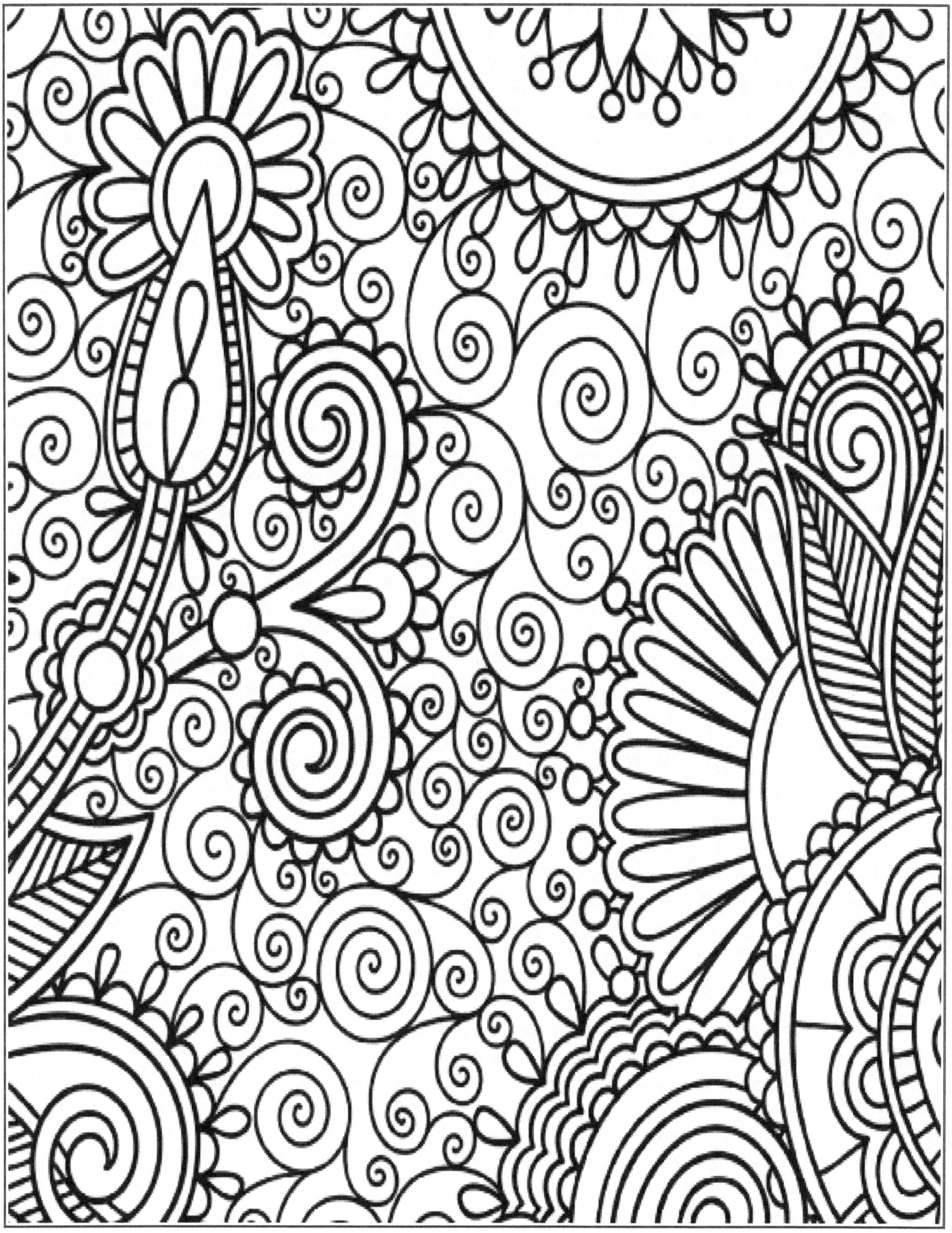

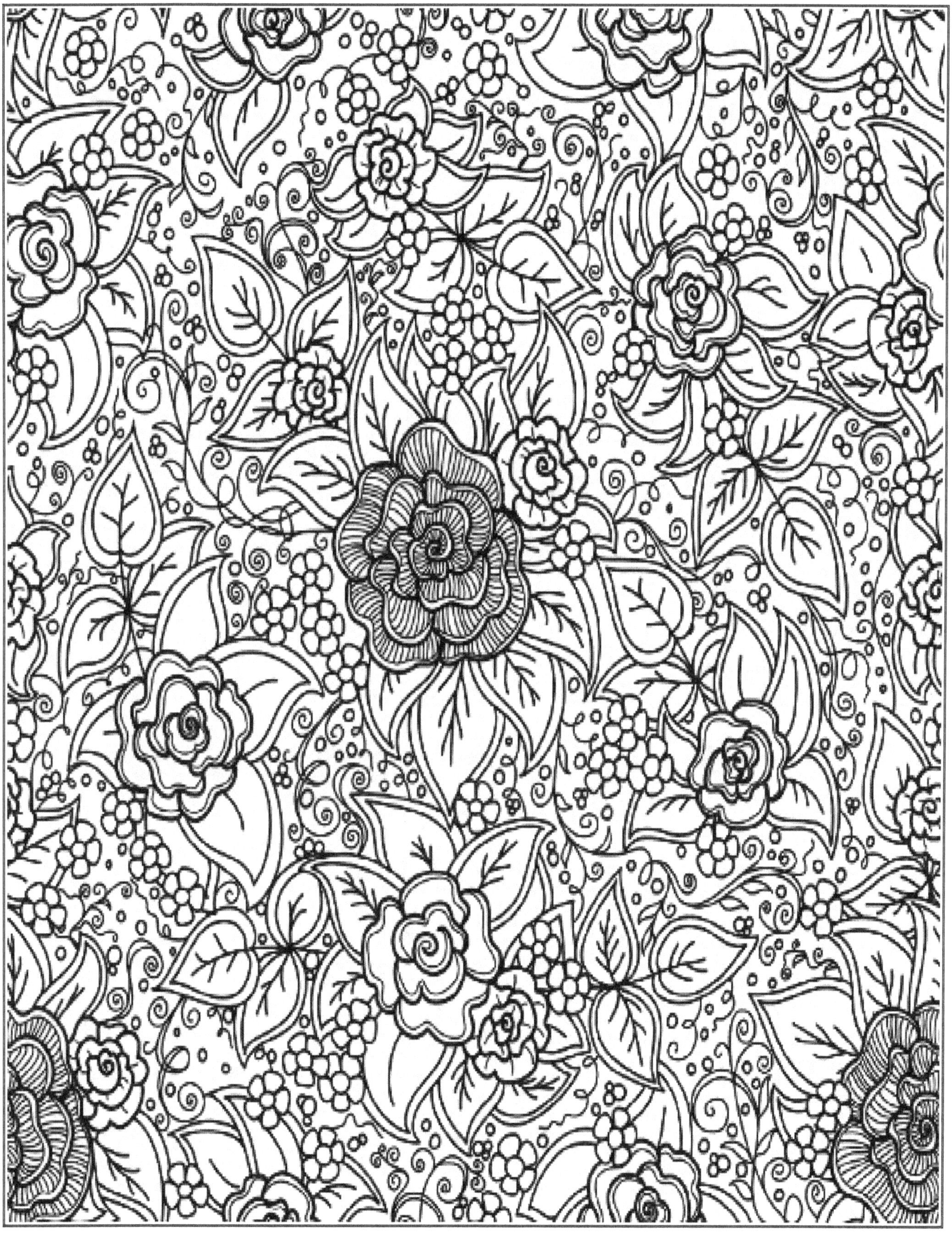

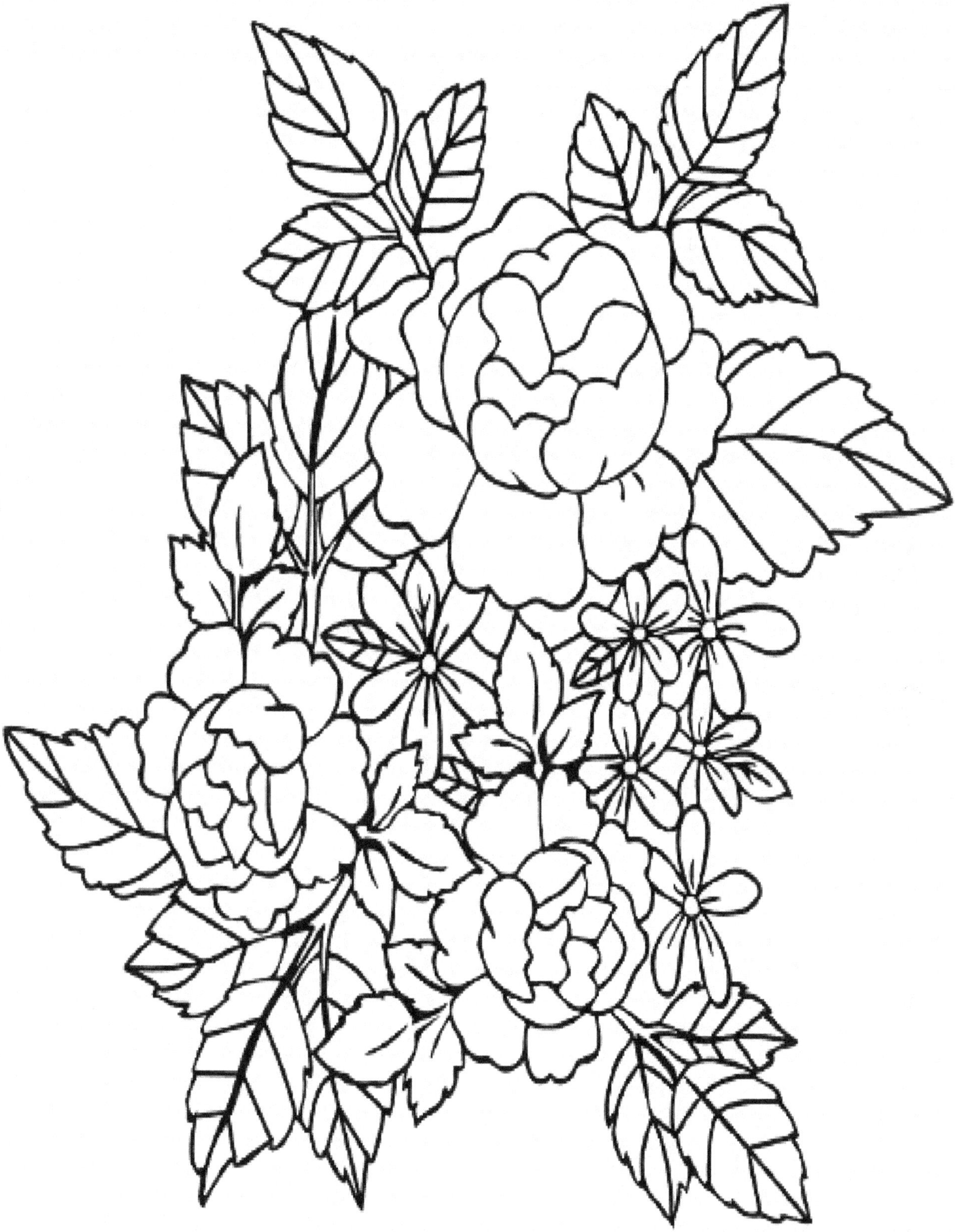

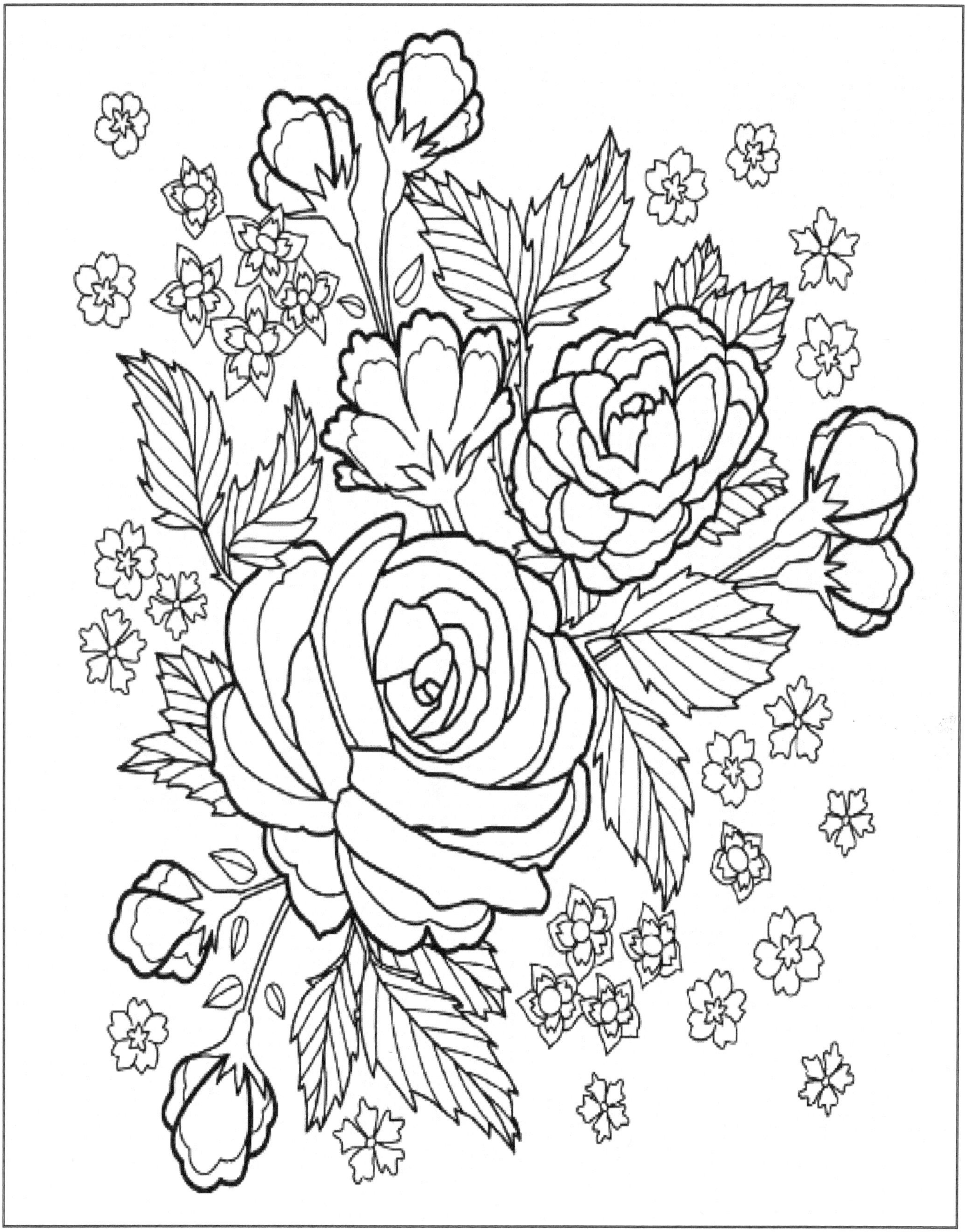

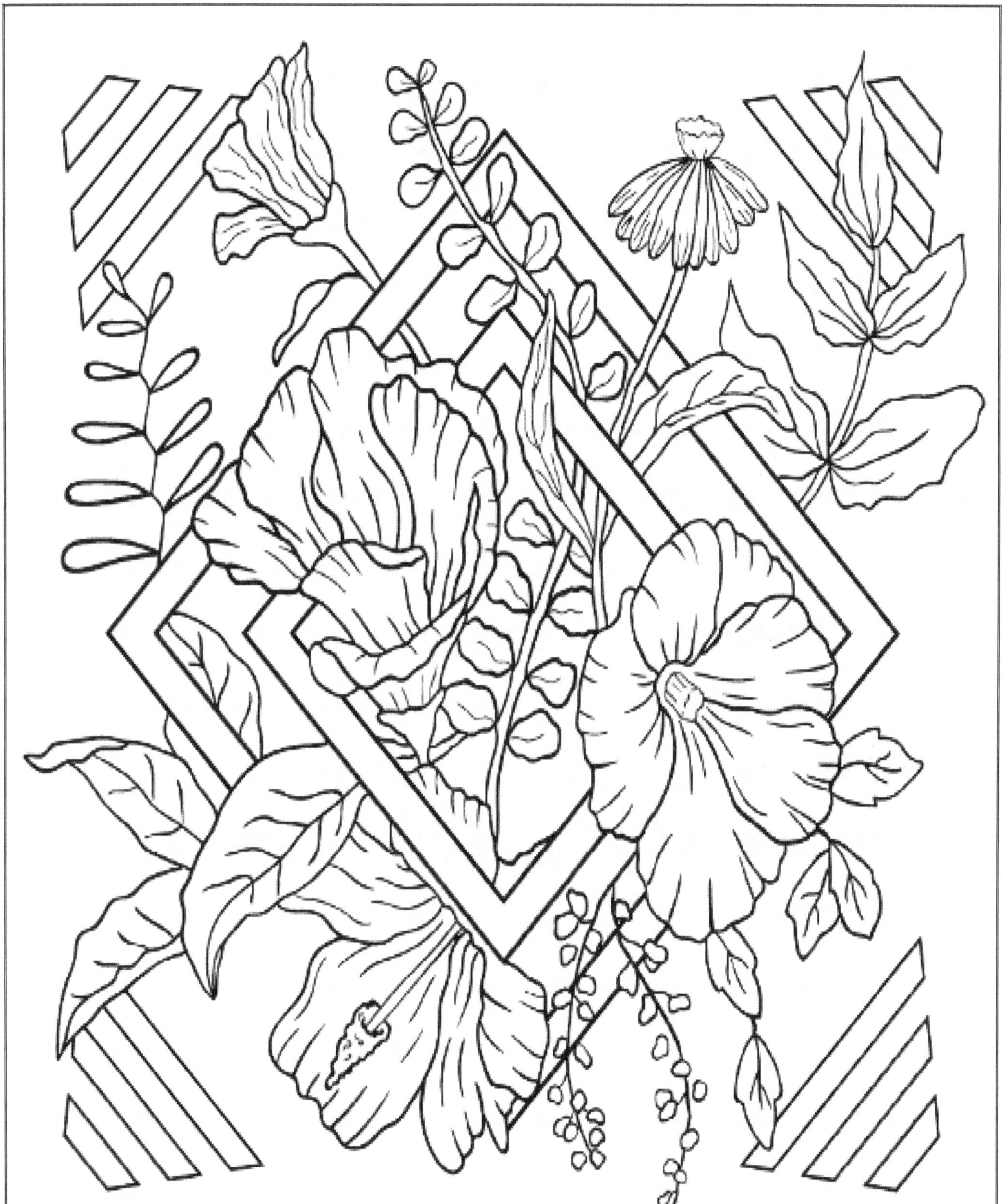

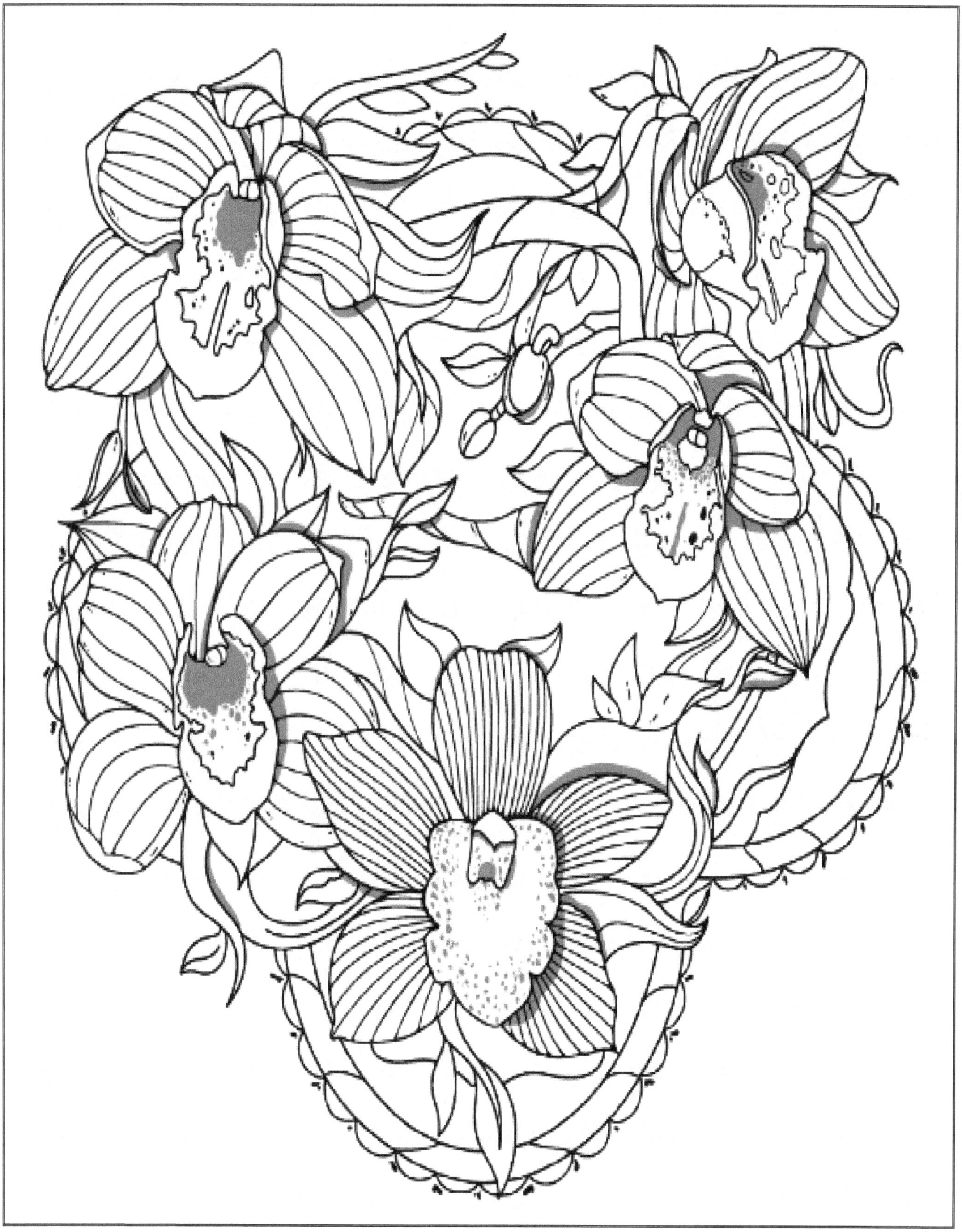

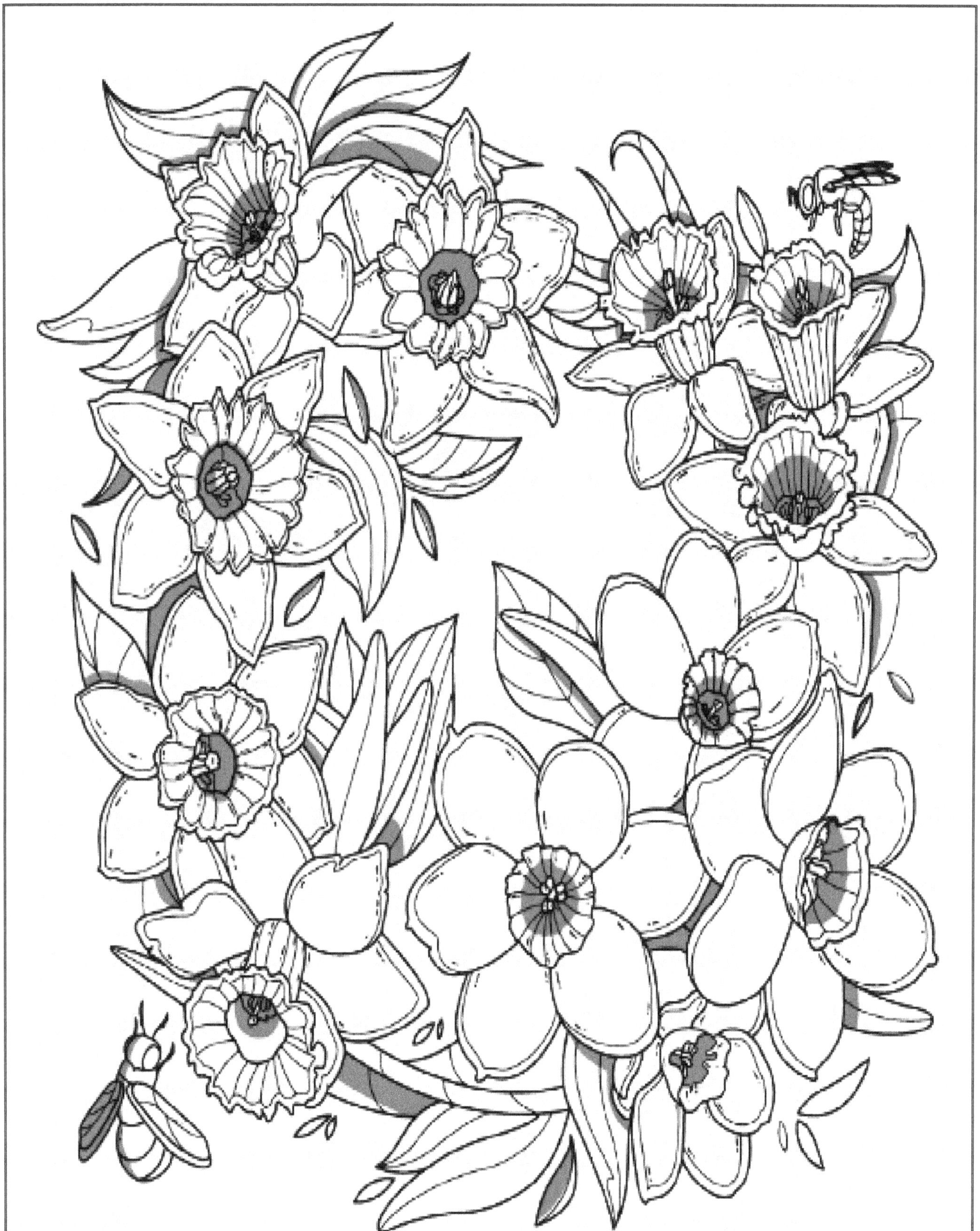

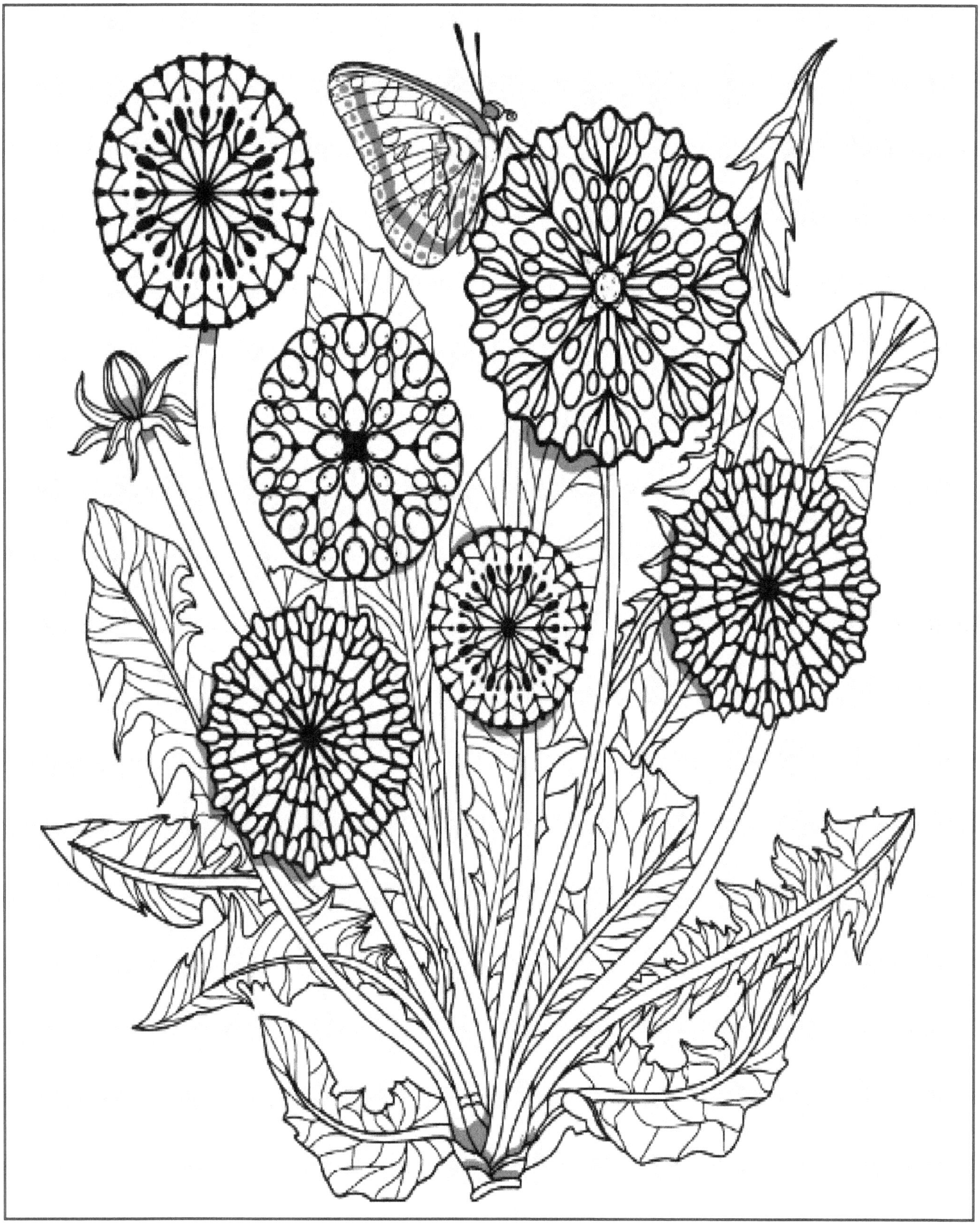

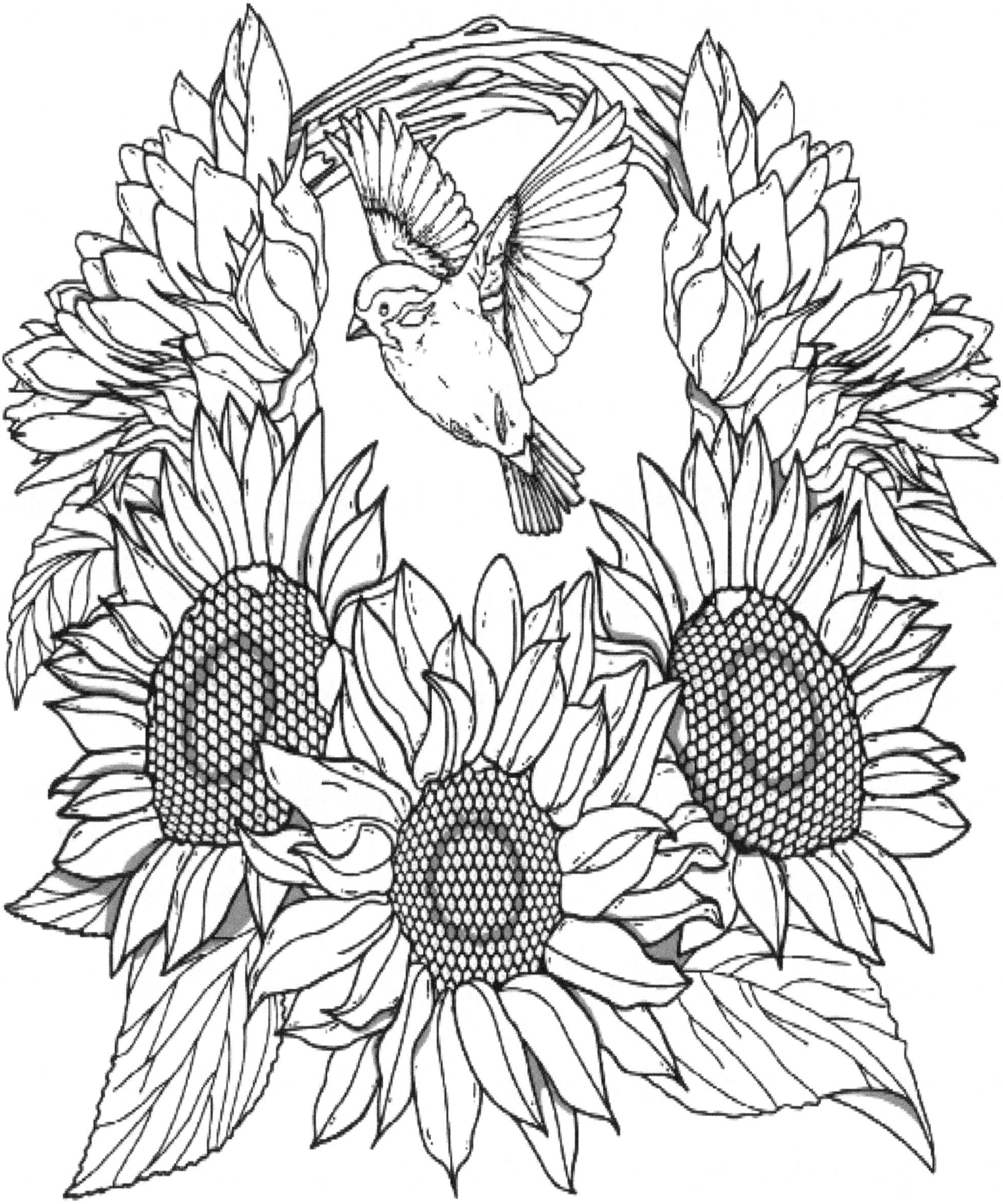

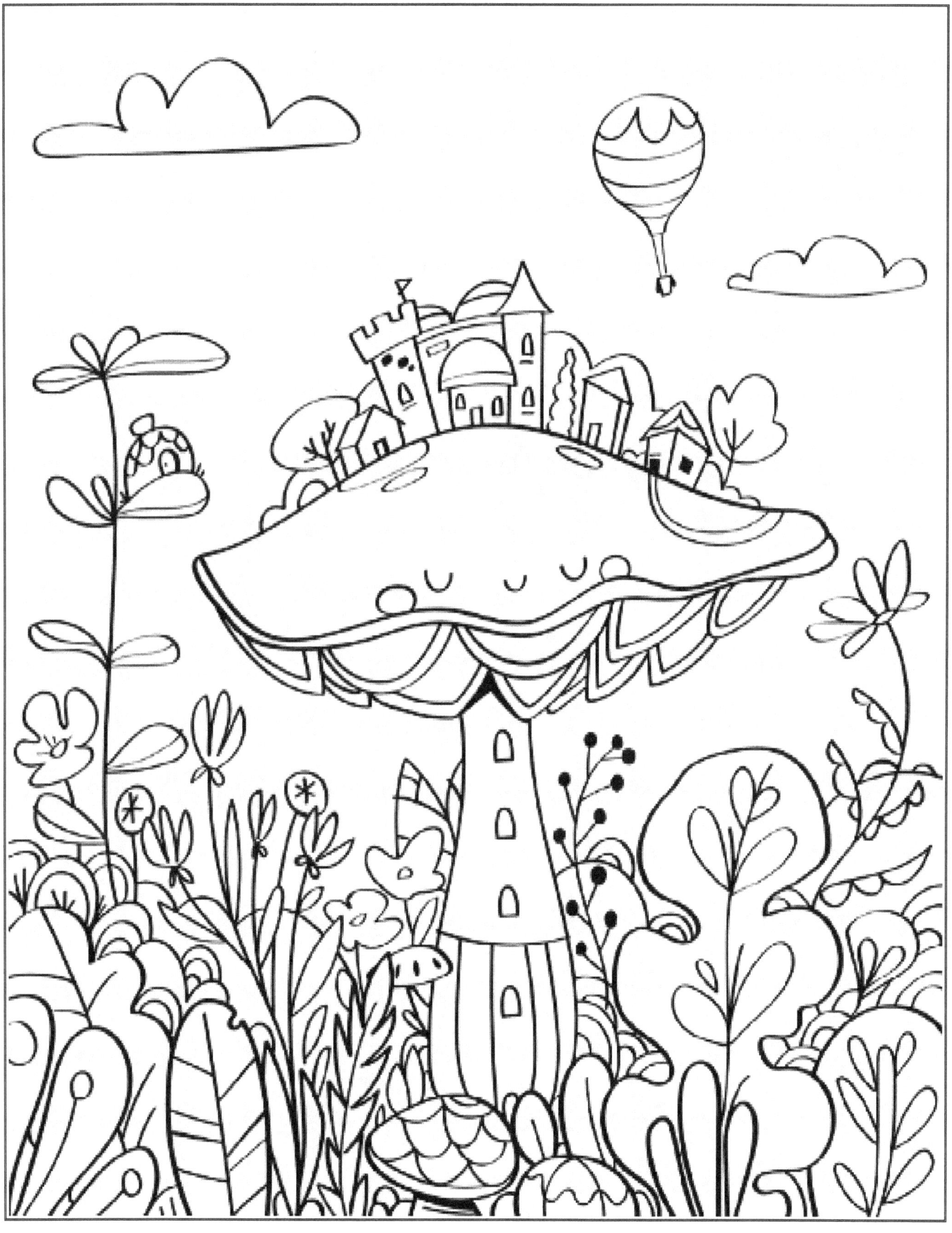

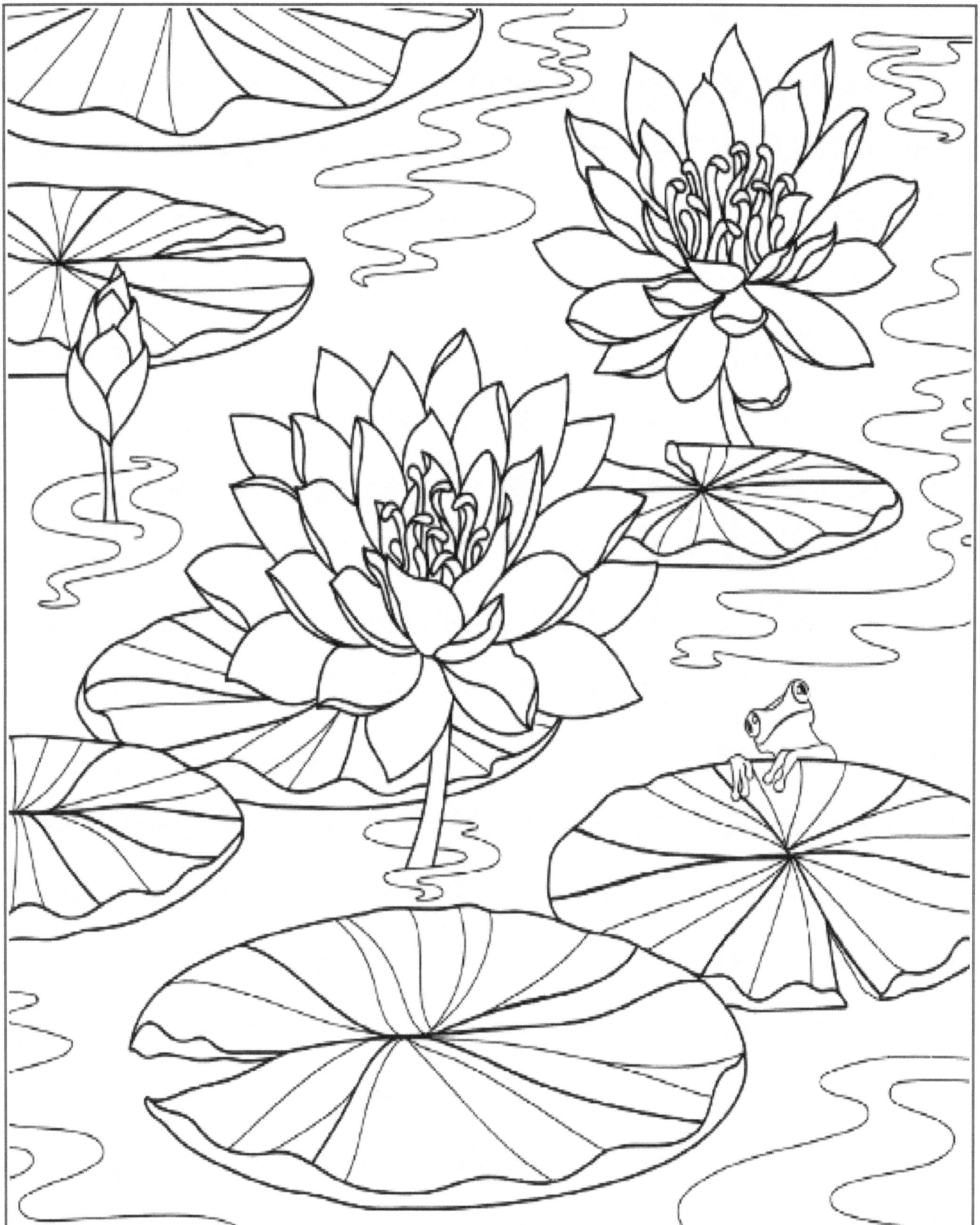

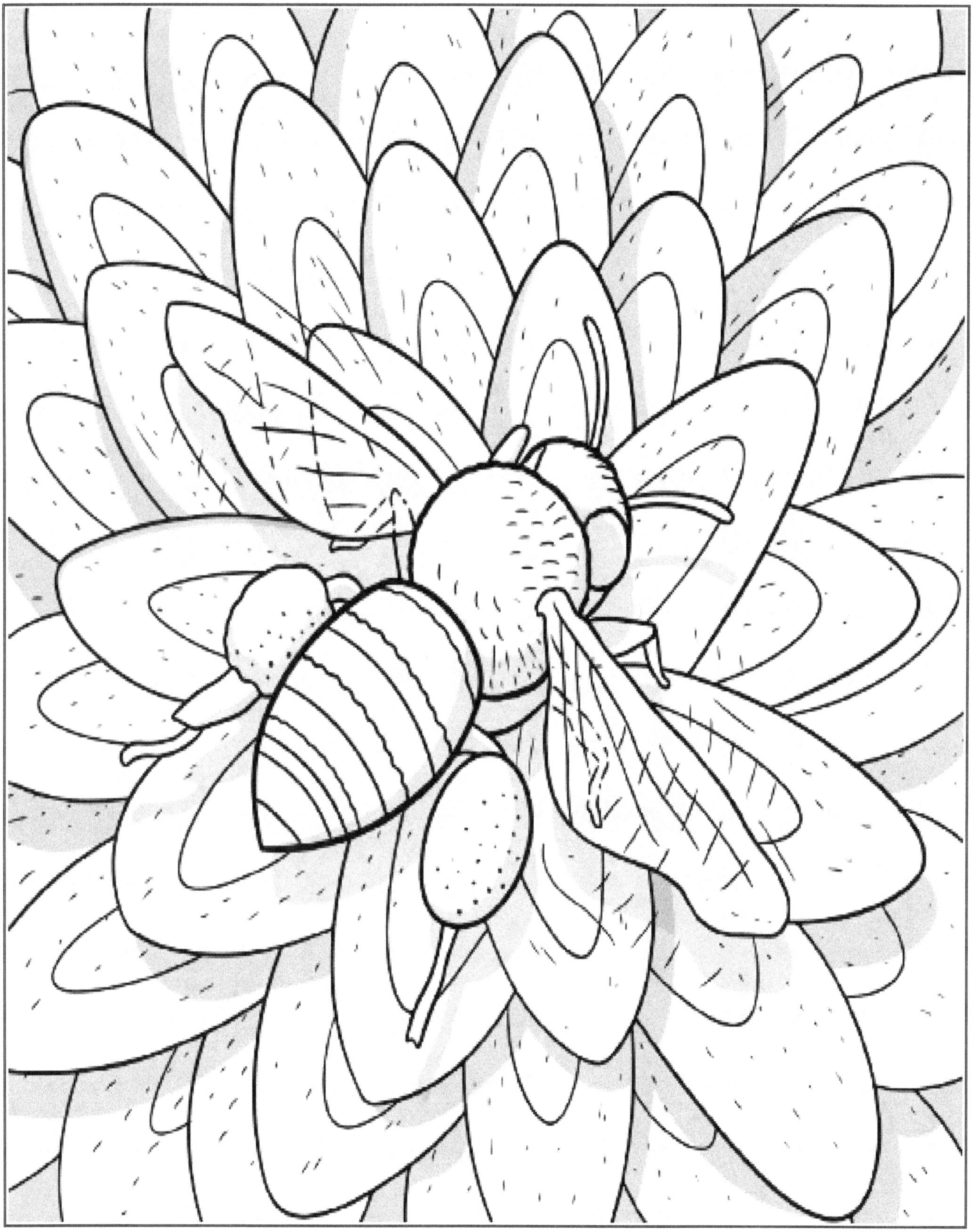

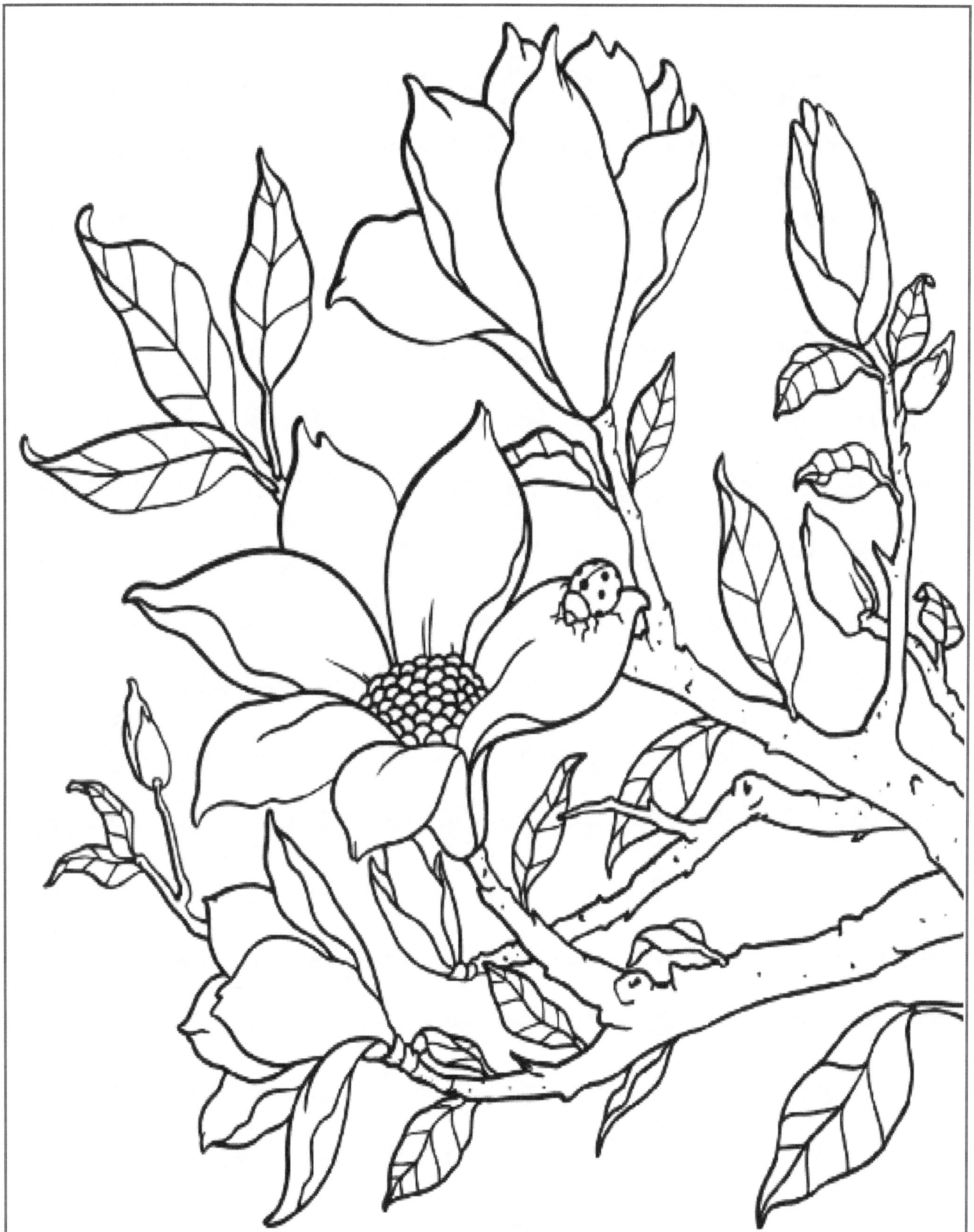

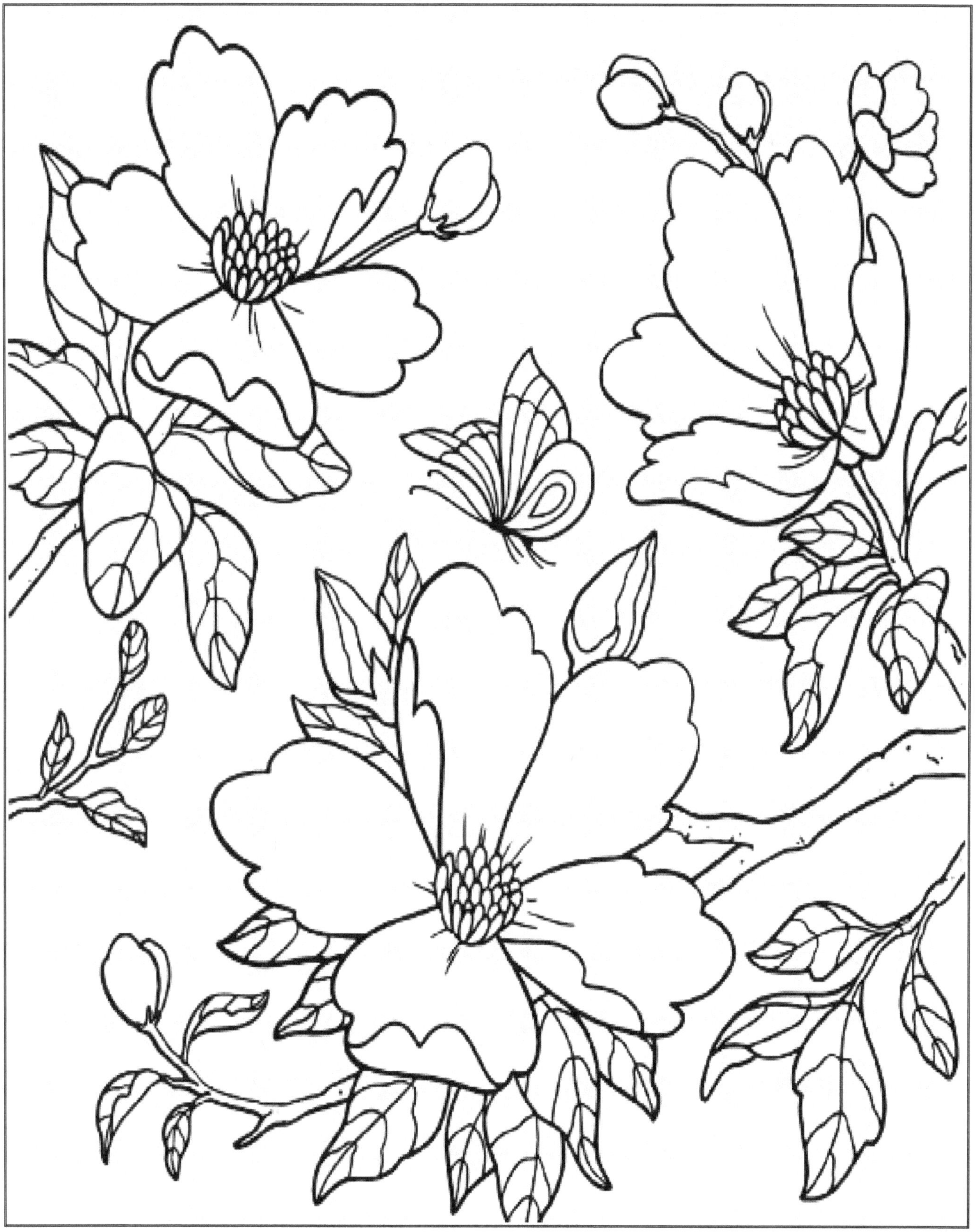

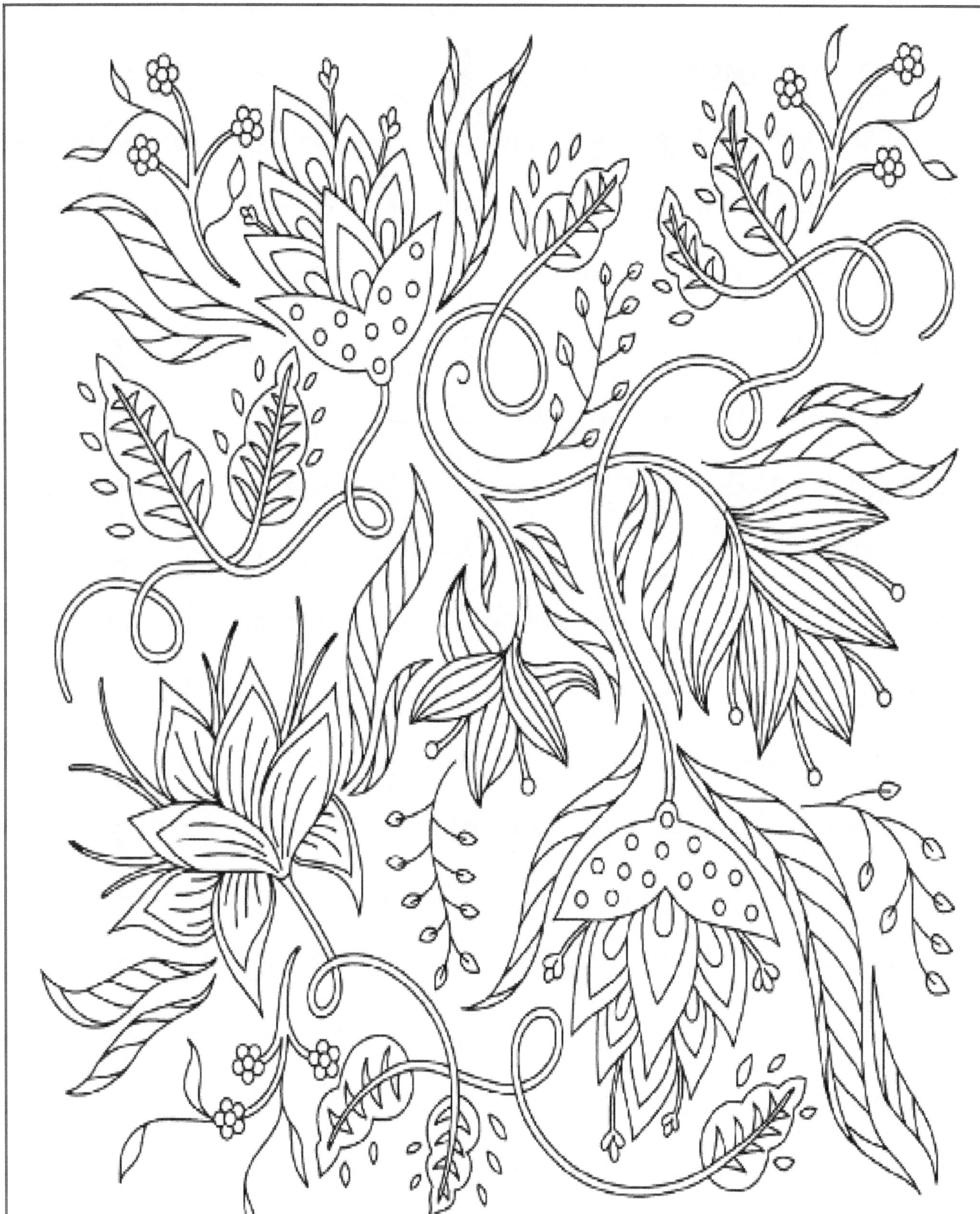

www.ingramcontent.com/pod-product-compliance
Lightning Source LLC
Chambersburg PA
CBHW081445220526
45466CB00008B/2509
* 9 7 8 1 6 7 8 0 0 7 9 9 7 *